Not In Vain

Ellis R. Shipp, M.D.

Not In Vain

Susan Evans McCloud

Bookcraft
Salt Lake City, Utah

Library of Congress Catalog Card Number: 84-70578
ISBN 0-88494-529-4

First Printing, 1984

Lithographed in the United States of America
PUBLISHERS PRESS
Salt Lake City, Utah

To my children

> *Heather, Jennie, Jared,*
> *Rebeccah, Morag, Mairi*

I hold their bright spirits as my
greatest treasures, my purest joys.
With Ellis I acknowledge the beauty
and privilege of being a mother.

If I can stop one heart from breaking,
I shall not live in vain;
If I can ease one life the aching,
Or cool one pain,

Or help one fainting robin
Unto his nest again,
I shall not live in vain.

Emily Dickinson

Contents

Preface

As early as 1980, while researching material for my second novel, I encountered the name of Dr. Ellis Shipp; not only the name but the haunting features looking out at me from old photographs. She was beautiful to look upon, and part of her beauty came from the clear intelligence in her face, the warm light in her eyes. The bits and snatches I learned about her I used in my public speaking; she was certainly someone women could emulate. It was not until the summer of 1983 that I was motivated to look further, to pull together the fragments that had been teasing at my mind, to discover and re-create the essence of a rare and remarkable woman.

Ellis Shipp's life brings a vital ray of illumination to the history of her time. Her accomplishments were significant. But more even than what she did is what she was. If, as George Sand said, "There is but one virtue—the eternal sacrifice of self," Ellis's triumphs in everyday living give us increased awareness of our own purpose and possibilities. In our day, which places such stress on woman's role and woman's fulfillment, Ellis Shipp's courage, commitment, and vision fall like sweet dew upon a desert.

I have felt the influence of her spirit as I worked; that inexplicable essence of a life that neither time nor the grave can totally dissipate nor dim. I rejoice that such women lived for us to follow; that there is still the sound of voices crying, "Be true to your divine nature, your proven destiny"; and that "self-fulfillment"—that pain-born child of exigency and self-will—will come as part of the purity and power that only women who truly magnify their womanhood will ever know.

In some small measure to present, to support, to reaffirm the thrilling substance of such a life—this has been my privilege. In one sense, Ellis Shipp needs no words spoken for her. She speaks eloquently for herself. It is our concern, rather, that we have ears to hear and hearts to understand.

1

Iowa Plains to Battle Creek

She was born on a clear, fine morning in January when the winter sun had just broken above the hills, flooding the frosted landscape with shafts of gold, transforming the frozen fields into gardens of treasure; diamonds that glinted and sparkled beneath the warm light. She was their first, and because she came at this magical moment her parents called her "sunshine"—a term of endearment which would grow to have more than one meaning in her life.

They named her Ellis after her mother's mother and marked the date of her birth as January 20, 1847, and the place simply somewhere in Davis County, Iowa. Her father, William Fletcher Reynolds, was twenty years old; her mother, Anna Hawley, just seventeen. Less than a year before, in February, they had been united as husband and wife. William, originally from Indiana, had cast his fortunes with the kindly, enterprising Hawley family, and was bound to them now with deeper ties.

William Hawley, Anna's father, was an able and powerful man. At nineteen he had cleared his own homestead in the Canadian wilderness. With an eye for timber he built his own log house,

squaring every log with his broadaxe, splitting and smoothing the
logs for the puncheon floor. He broke the yoke of oxen his father
had given him and built a cart, coopered kegs and buckets, and was
ready when the maple sap season came in February. According to
the account of one of his daughters, Sarah Ellis, his enterprise won
him profit, as well as the admiration of his family:

> When the sugar season was over and his father and brothers
> had time from their own labors of sugar making for a breathing
> spell, his parents sent Henry, his youngest brother, over to see how
> Bill was getting along. Henry came and he saw, and he returned
> home with a tale to tell.
> "Why, Father," he said, "Bill has as much sugar as you and all
> five boys have made!"
> "But he couldn't do it," the old man exclaimed. "We've all
> worked like beavers all season."
> And then Henry explained how he had done it — that instead
> of carrying the sap to camp by a yoke over the shoulders from
> which the sap buckets are suspended at each end, he had a cart and
> kegs and made the steers do the carrying for him, and accomplished
> as much as six men could do by the usual method. He sold his sugar
> that year in Buffalo for one thousand dollars, and that put him on
> the upgrade toward comparative independence.[1]

Elsie Ellis Smith, his wife, was well matched with her husband.
They had planted a field of flax and, after the reaping, she spun
and wove it into linen, hand-sewing sheets, pillowslips, towels, and
underclothing, making the hemp into men's wear. She set up her
little spinning wheel in the sugar camp where she could be close by
her husband, working each night until nearly midnight while he
"sugared off." She kept geese and made soft feather beds and pil-
lows. William built her a milk house over the spring with a smooth
stone floor where water three inches deep flowed through and out
a lower vent. She kept her crooks of milk to cool here. He even
rigged up a little wheel turned by water power which was attached
to the churn dasher and did her churning for her.

As the years passed they continued to prosper. William held
the office of high sheriff in the district and together they owned
and ran an English-style inn boasting its own baker, barber, boot-
black, and bar. Entertaining was a way of life, almost a religion
with them. Both English and Canadian gentry would come by the

sleigh load to stay and visit several days at a time. Then Ellis would bake her mince pies by the fifties and make doughnuts by the barrel for her hungry guests. There would be games and dancing and story-telling and Ellis, bright-eyed, would move among her friends wearing one of the pretty silk dresses she took such delight in.

But after almost twenty years of such living, and bearing and nearly raising their family, the political climate in Canada became tense and dangerous as revolts broke out against the King's men, and stern government investigations were organized to discover whose sympathies were republican, whose for the Crown.

This, combined with tales of the Oregon country, tempting reports of the climate and resources there, caused several of the Hawleys to change their allegiance and set out for homes in the unspoiled American frontier. William drove west on the Talbot Road to Detroit, stayed in mid-Michigan two or three years, then settled in Davis County, Iowa, where their last child, James E., was born in 1840, eleven years after Anna's birth. Here, with the same industry and determination, they built another comfortable home and their children, as they married, settled near them. Now Anna had married a William of her own, and given them this exquisite, dark-eyed granddaughter.

Ellis couldn't have been more warmly received and cared for. She recorded her own first feelings and impressions:

> My earliest recollections may be compared to the first feeble fluttering of the tiniest bird's wing, and yet the beautiful impress remains. The gentle pressure of loving arms, fond smiles of soothing tenderness, the sweet music of subdued voices, the bended forms over my little crib—the soothing words, the lullaby songs of mother and grandmother as they swayed to and fro in the dear old rocking chair—Oh, those blessed ones trying to ease and still the cries of a babe![2]

While yet an infant Ellis had a close brush with death. A doctor who had been called to treat her for some slight ailment administered an overdose of paregoric. Anna, frantic, summoned her father, calling him away from his work. He took the child from her mother's protective arms into his own and carried her out into the open air. He swung her back and forth and shook her roughly, all the while calling to her urgently.

"Ellis, we will not let you die," he told her. "You must stay with us, Ellis, you must live! You must live!"

Somehow the baby responded to his efforts, to the pull of his love, of his own strong will. This incident, related to Ellis often during her childhood, became the foundation for a powerful union between her grandfather and herself.

They were altogether a close-knit family. Some of her uncles were not much older than Ellis; little James was only seven when she was born. Some of her cousins were close in age as well, Susan Ellis being only a year her senior. But the closeness went deeper than conditions and circumstances. There was a basic code of love and loyalty among them, all pulling for one and one for all. Ellis wrote in later years:

> Since the dawn of intelligence have I been supremely grateful to my Father in Heaven for my earthly parentage — that He sent my spirit to such a lineage. Truly, to be well-born is the greatest heritage of humanity and to come where one is wanted and not under protest as so many spirits do.[3]

Sometime during the early years of Ellis's childhood her mother gave birth to a little son who contracted smallpox during an epidemic and lived but a short while.

"This was my first recollection of sorrow," Ellis stated. "My stricken parents, the little form carried away in a box. How I wondered, how I cried. I could not comprehend."[4]

It is at this time that the gentle, heroic nature of Ellis's father came into play. Apparently he had received an early form of vaccination against the disease which, though scarring his handsome face, had made him immune. Now, and for the rest of his life, it became his custom to go about among the severly afflicted — to places where no one else had courage to go — rendering tender care and comfort. He healed many, but he also sat with the dying, then prepared their bodies for burial. Often he made their funeral caskets as well and comforted those left behind to mourn.

Ellis called him "the staff and stay of his home, the mediator and peacemaker of every situation."[5] She stated, in a brief biography of her father, that he had been made an orphan at an early age. Perhaps his own sufferings increased his compassion for others who suffered. Whatever the influences or impulses behind it, Ellis frequently praised her father's kind, sympathetic, and generous nature.

During the first few years of Ellis's childhood a phenomenon appeared in the neighborhood. Long trains of refugees in ox-drawn wagons appeared against the horizon, filing along the quiet Iowa roads, past rich farmlands so much like the ones they had left behind. A man on horseback rode from farm to farm frantically warning, "The Mormons are coming! Don't open your gates. Don't let them camp on your lands. Why, they'll steal everything they can lay their hands on. They're lazy and immoral. They can't even have a drink of water from my place. They must drive through straight on out of our community."[6]

The Hawleys listened, but found themselves more curious than frightened. They all came down to the gate to watch the Mormons go by. Their hearts were touched by the pain they saw in the wayfarers' faces. Ellis Hawley stood with her arm around little Jimmy, who sat on the fence post. William waited to catch her eye, then lifted his eyebrows in question. She slowly nodded.

He strode forward and threw his wide double gates open, inviting the strangers to drive in their wagons and rest. He offered them free pasturage for their cattle, water, wood, and provisions for themselves. For three days the grateful people remained there — bathing, washing their clothing, restocking the precious foodstuffs to maintain their lives. But what did they have to share with these generous people? What could they give in return? There was only one thing and it was priceless: their testimony of the true gospel of Jesus Christ.

Yet this first contact did not convert either the Hawleys or Ellis's parents. They went about the affairs of their own business, unaware of the dark currents that moved around them. Most of their neighbors had banded together against the Mormons, denying them even a cool drink from one of their wells, then bragging about their harsh treatment, supporting each other. They resented the Reynolds and Hawleys for not joining in. Even more they resented William's defense of the Mormons, clearing their names when they were unjustly accused of some theft or other dishonesty.

Quietly, mysteriously things started to happen: a gap in his fence line where stray stock wandered through and destroyed his crops; an unexplained fire in one of his outbuildings; his own cattle and horses run off where he couldn't find them. It was all very gradual, but so was the family's conversion. Early in 1851 William and Elsie Ellis Hawley were baptized—secretly, in the woods, in the dead of night. Ezra T. Benson performed the ordinance; their sixteen-year-old son, Asa, stood as the only witness.

At this time Ellis was just turning four years old. The date when her own parents, William and Anna, were baptized has not been recorded. From all accounts it followed soon after the Hawley's baptism. And now, of course, came another natural decision.

They offered their farms for sale but, not surprisingly, they could find no buyers. The local farmers—not so long ago neighbors and friends—whispered among themselves, "Why should we buy? When they leave and join with those Mormons we can get every bit of their property just for taxes."

Their prosperity was like spilt milk now, like sand slipping through their fingers. Father Hawley obtained a wood contract in Henderson County, Illinois. This was a move east, across the Mississippi, back where the Mormons were coming from. His two young sons, Ben and Asa, worked with him. And so did his son-in-law, William Reynolds. The two men worked well together. This was not their first, nor would it be their last, new venture.

Ellis didn't remember the Mississippi. But she remembered the River Henderson. Its clear, rippling water was a delight to her. When she grew tired or fussy her father would carry her down to the shoreline. Her tears would disappear and she would be lost in the powerful beauty of the clear, running water. She remembered playing along a high bank and watching the men down below work in the timber, fell the tall trees, and hew the broad logs, the sharp bark of their axes echoing through the still air. One by one the logs floated down the river, and one by one the preparations were made.

With the profit made from the lumber they purchased excellent outfits in Kanesville. William, a skilled carpenter and wheelwright, constructed with his family's assistance his own sturdy wagons, five in all, securely boxed, intricately fitted together, covered with strong, closely woven canvas that moisture couldn't penetrate. There was a light spring wagon as well, called a carriage, horse- or mule-drawn. The larger wagons were drawn by at least two oxen, three or four if heavily laden.

The family at this time consisted of William and Elsie Ellis Hawley, their three youngest sons Asa, Benjamin, and James; Mary Webb Hawley, the widow of their oldest son, William Henry; and her small five-year-old daughter, Susan Ellis. There was also Anna Hawley Reynolds, her husband William, their two children, Ellis and George, and at least one brother of William's, Levi Reynolds. They joined Captain Snow's company and William Hawley was appointed a captain of fifty.

The first day of the journey dawned gray and chill with a drizzling rain. The confinement of wagon-box quarters seemed dull and uncomfortable. But day-by-day adjustments came as the experience expanded and they were moving, the dream at last taking on reality.

Ellis's father walked the greater part of the journey, often stooping to pick up pretty rocks and shells to present to his little daughter, who responded enthusiastically. Five-year-old Ellis rode beside her mother who, in spite of having baby George to tend to, kept her hands busy knitting, mending, and sewing on buttons. This industry was not lost on the child who watched her, whose sensitive heart stored up the impressions of these early days.

Seldom do we see that trek reflected through the eyes of a child. Ellis left a picture of continuous wonder and new adventure. The children, largely unaware of the ills and fears of their parents, drank in the beauty and responded to the myriad of new sensations.

> The children—how carefree and happy, walking and running, lending a helping hand at camping time, looking for sticks of wood for fires or, when not one little stick could we find, gathering buffalo chips in baskets and aprons.—Why, I can almost taste yet the delicious johnnycake and maple syrup my dear mother turned out from that old-fashioned bake kettle. How delicious and nutritious it was with the fresh rich milk my dear father stripped from old Spot, our favorite cow we could not leave behind.
>
> What a wonderful development in the beautiful things of na-

ture were the far-stretching prairie lands. At times a tall, towering tree made us dance with delight. And oh, the glorious sunsets and the welcome sunrise, the gorgeous tints of the sky, the mellow haze of the hilltops, sometimes the fluttering of a bird's wing, the sight of its tinted plummage. Each morning I wakened with pleasant expectations of newly-shaped roadways; now and then a trickling stream or bubbling spring where we had a cool drink or, perhaps, a deep muddy gulch which, after having passed over safely, I would feel so thankful my father was safe after his precarious clinging to the wagon gear, and that my dear mother had kept herself and brother and me from falling over the front onto the backs of the oxen. I would shout with delight over a Johnny-jump-up, the wild pinks, the sweet william, and every tiny spike of green. . . ."[7]

There was one special high wagon with slanting staves painted bright blue. Ellis and Susan, Polly Lamb, and Helen Winters would struggle over the sides and tumble inside, reaching eager hands down in the cracker barrel, dipping fingers into the rich, sweet maple syrup. No grown-up ever chided or denied them. At night around the campfires there were stories, old songs, and sometimes dancing to the strains of her Uncle Levi's violin. And for Ellis there was the extra treat of riding, as the long day closed, in the light swift carriage with her grandparents, snuggled safely between them, going before the train to scout out a camp site where there would be wood and water and feed for the animals. The speed seemed exhilarating, almost magical after the tedious ploddings and joltings of the day's ride.

One day as he walked along beside his oxen William Reynolds discovered two discarded wagon tires. Thinking they might prove useful he stopped to get them, securing them to the outside of the wagon, where they rattled and banged against the box, jangling and out of beat with the plodding gait of the oxen and the low, protesting creaks of the tall wheels. Even Ellis found the sound annoying, much preferring the "gee" and "haw" of the drivers, the sharp cracking of their long, black whips and the crunching of the coarse stones beneath the weight of the wagons. For miles the endless prairie spread before them in a long, unbroken plain, far past her vision, seeming to her young mind as if it must stretch to the very ends of the world.

At night when they stopped to make camp the wagons would

form in two half circles with openings left between the sections. The tongues of the wagons would point outward, each front wheel lapping the hind wheel of the next wagon. This made an effective corral for the cattle and oxen, as well as a fortification for the people. A sentinel was placed to guard each opening, reporting every hour from ten at night until five in the morning.

"Ten o'clock," his voice would call out in the stillness. "Ten o'clock and all is well . . . all is well . . . " to echo over the sleeping wagons.

Captain Snow's company had crossed Iowa and, following the north branch of the Platte River, were well into Nebraska when tragedy struck. Rebecca Winters, a lifelong friend and neighbor of the family, had been stricken with cholera and was now dying. It was grandmother Hawley who nursed her, staying constantly by her side, doing all she could. The camp did not move — one day, two days — waiting, hopelessly now, for what was to come.

Then on the third day clouds of gray dust rose off in the distance and with them the dull thud of many horses. Helpless, they watched the Indians come nearer, draw up outside the wagons, and dismount. The Indians' bodies and faces were smeared with paint in gaudy war colors, their aspect angry and threatening.

They demanded food, tobacco, and whiskey. The pioneers' supplies were sadly depleted. There was no way they could meet the Indians' demands and hope to sustain their own lives for the rest of the journey. Vainly their leaders reasoned with the warriors; there was no budging them. The Indians wanted food — they would have it one way or another.

At last William Hawley tried his hand, using all his persuasive powers to turn them. They only became more menacing and hostile. He looked off for a quiet moment, then gazed keenly back at the Indians who stood watching. "Well, come on then, follow me," he told them.

He led the way back to the wagon where Rebecca Winters lay dying. He threw aside the cover; dark faces gazed in. One by one they looked upon the woman — pale, hollow-cheeked, eyes wide and sightless. There was silence for a long moment. Then the

Indians screamed, a sound that shivered along the backbone. Frightened, they turned; they spurred their animals onward, going back to where they had come as fast as they could.

That night Rebecca Winters died. Grandmother Hawley took from her own chest of drawers material for the burial clothing. She and Anna sewed together through the dark hours. Ellis stood in the shivering night air beside her father, holding the lantern high so he could work, performing his own act of love and service. Other men dug through the hard, unyielding surface a grave — a shallow scar on the prairie's broad surface.

"Dig deeper," William Hawley instructed. Ellis remembered standing beside her grandfather, listening while he encouraged the tired men. "We will have one grave no beast can harm. Dig deeper, boys, deeper!"[8]

When the time for the burial came, William Reynolds brought forth his offering. He had chiseled Rebecca's name on the old wagon tires. They would no longer clank tiredly at the wagon side. As he adjusted the circling bands into the soil he quietly stated, "This shall be the means of identifying this grave in years to come."[9] Time would tell how true was his prophecy.

At last, after months of travel, the journey ended. The company reached Echo Canyon, crossed Big and Little mountains, then stood at the mouth of Emigration Canyon and beheld the magnificent valley spread out below. On October 9, 1852, the train pulled into Salt Lake City; Brother Snow's company disbanded, and the members were free to go their own ways.

The Hawleys, the Reynolds, and several others — including the husband and children of Rebecca Winters — drove south across the mountains to Utah Valley. It is interesting to note that Hiram Winters, husband of Rebecca, had been one of the members of Zions Camp. He settled near the Hawley family with his daughter, Helen — Ellis's close friend — his sons, Oscar and Alonzo; Oscar's wife, Mary Ann Winters; and Mary Ann's mother, the wife of Parley P. Pratt. William Hawley's daughter, Sarah Ellis, in her history of the family states: "It was your grandma Hawley who loved Rebecca's children and mothered them, and whom they loved like a mother all her life."[10]

William Hawley stopped his teams at the Point of the Mountain, the elevation point which divided Salt Lake County from Utah County. The expanse of the virgin valley spread out below; the encircling foothills, flaming with autumn colors, the blue freshwater lake to the west, here and there a stand of timber, a bright stain of color framed against the brown earth and the clear sky.

Carefully he studied the map before him and determined to settle as nearly in sight of that lake as he could. Not at Lehi, for he could see that the canyon currents would keep that spot constantly windy: he didn't much care what the weather was — as long as the wind didn't blow. He went on, bypassing American Fork, too. He wanted a spot on the lower slopes of those eastern mountains. They came to the town called Battle Creek.

At the foot of Mount Timpanogos, the city looked east to the mountains and west to Utah Lake. To the north and south lay the fertile bench lands, with hills and then higher mountains stretching to distance. There was good soil here and an abundance of water, and beauty to fill the heart and the searching eye. The Reynolds and Hawleys bought lands along the bottoms, a little below the town on the country road. Their first neighbors were Lewis Robinson and Daniel H. Wells.

They lived there peacefully and happily for eight brief, but very full, years. Even Ellis herself in later years looked back on those early pioneer efforts as wonderfully heroic, something out of a noble past that would not return.

> Busy mothers planned and worked in these hastily-erected temporary homes in what was then called "the bottoms" — an expanse of level lands where were found springs of pure fresh water and abundant grass for cattle. Some of the crude little homes were but "dugouts," with several steps under ground. Nearly all had but mud floors — no sawmills, not even a nail, little wooden pegs in place of tacks. Strips of white cloth were tacked over open spaces for windows and blankets hung up for doors. And yet what rejoicing gratitude for their shelters, with their large open fireplaces filled with blazing fires for cold mornings, and the bed of coals when our mothers prepared the good foods. What pioneer can forget the iron kettle hanging from the iron crane in the upper part of the fireplace? These things were luxuries to mothers who for months had pre-

pared meals over smoking campfires of sagebrush and buffalo chips. And I must not forget that venerable bake kettle, the reservoir of cream biscuits and johnnycake, and sometimes for a real treat when company came or when some dear one had a birthday, the delicious cornmeal pudding which (when the hens laid) must be made with eggs and always with sugar and rich milk and baked slowly many hours.

In those days work was the watchword! The oxen were kept busy hauling stone and timber; the few farming implements, plows, harrows, spades and hoes and shovels, soon were brightened with working the heretofore unturned soil. I well remember my own little gardon spot in the rear and my dear flower garden in front of the humble home. As I recall those early days I do not remember being hungry, but I do wonder how our dear parents gained their livelihood and provided so generously for their families. The people were one in faith and works, all as one united family, ever willing to help each other and to divide their pittances where they were needed.[11]

Battle Creek had first been settled in 1850 by a few families sent by Brigham Young and led by George S. Clark. By 1851 the name had been unofficially changed, somehow, to Pleasant Grove. In a letter from Brother Clark to Brigham reporting his progress, and dated late winter of 1851, he wrote in his heading "Pleasant Grove, Utah." In March of the same year the name appears in the first official Church record written by Thomas Bullock.

There was reason for the name. A lush grove of cottonwoods some forty feet high spread like a stately oasis in the midst of the alkaline sage. The early settlers cherished "The Grove" and were jealous of it, imposing in unwritten law a fine of fifty dollars for malicious or selfish destruction of any of the trees. Not until 1862 when the raging flood waters of Grove Creek overran their bounds was there any serious sacrifice of the lovely grove.

By the time Ellis's family arrived in the city an LDS ward had already been organized. George Clark was appointed first bishop; his counselors were Duncan MacArthur and James Dunn. There were nearly 100 people in the settlement as well as 21 horses, 1 mule, 46 cows, 4 swine, 32 young cattle, 87 oxen, 27 sheep—and 25 wagons. Two hundred fifty acres of land had been planted with corn, oats, barley, potatoes, and buckwheat. School was held in the

Stevens home and in April 1852, Pleasant Grove was designated School District No. 5 of Utah County.

There was much to do and the Reynolds and Hawleys fit quickly into the ongoing scheme. Work on the first schoolhouse was begun in September; they arrived in time to help complete it. It was built of handmade adobes and logs all cut and shaped by hand. The desks and benches were large log slabs with holes bored in each end and sticks fitted into the holes for legs. The first roll of pupils in the school numbered only a dozen, with Ben and Asa Hawley among the group. It would be a few more years yet before Ellis would go to school.

In the spring of 1853 Henson Walker was chosen to replace George Clark as bishop. Clark had been appointed to take a company of fifty families to help organize counties further south. When later Duncan MacArthur, one of his counselors, left for Mount Pleasant, William Hawley bought his holdings and lands, dividing the properties among his sons and living on MacArthur lands for the rest of his life.

Grandpa Hawley and his son-in-law, William Reynolds, built the first grist mill in the settlement, as well as an early molasses mill. Both had a phenomenal gift for building. William Hawley constructed the first bridge across the Provo River. Ellis's father constructed a turning lathe where he made and mended chairs, rolling pins, and potato mashers, all from native mahogany. He built Christmas toys to delight the children, even Easter eggs for their mothers to decorate.

The outbreak of the Walker War that summer caused overnight changes in the settlers' lives. Brigham Young instructed the people to build forts for better protection. Each family was assigned a lot inside the fort. This meant taking down the logs and adobes and rebuilding their cabins within the fort. Even the schoolhouse was torn down and built again inside the walls. The Reynolds and Hawley houses stood side by side on the north end of the fort, with Ben Hawley's house on the other side of Anna and William's.

To the children much of this was an adventure, and the Pleasant Grove fort was a remarkable place. The walls were built of rock two and a half feet thick, three—in some places five—feet high. The homes were built just inside the structure and a road extended the entire way around the four center blocks of the fort. Across the street from each home stood an individual family barn and in the square made by the barns was a community corral. But the most unique thing about this fort was its water system. Suzanna Mae Clark Grua in her history of Pleasant Grove describes it:

> A small box flume carried water from a spring east of town into the fort and then extended all the way around the fort on the front boundary of each home lot. At each home there was an opening in the flume where a cover could be lifted and the water dipped out for culinary purposes. The cover was always replaced so that the water was kept clean at all times. All stock was watered at troughs outside the fort and separate from the culinary system, which was a model for those early times.[12]

The fort served to unite the people and spur community growth and cooperation.

In January 1855, when Ellis was turning eight years old, Pleasant Grove became an incorporated city. Its government was set up with a mayor, four aldermen and nine councilors. Henson Walker became the first mayor; William J. Hawley one of his aldermen. In the spring of the same year work was begun on the first meetinghouse. William Reynolds was part of the building committee, a position which carried great responsibility.

George A. Smith visited Pleasant Grove in September 1855 and wrote:

> The Saints in Pleasant Grove have begun a meetinghouse sixty feet long and thirty-six feet wide, with a basement story ten feet high which can be used for storing large amounts of grain and vegetables. Adobe work is now fourteen feet high and walls two and a half feet thick. Bishop Walker informs me he expects the building to be completely enclosed in a month. It speaks well for the people, setting a pattern of union, energy, and perseverance worthy of larger towns.[13]

That year the men were not busy harvesting as they should have been. Grasshoppers had destroyed nearly all their crop. Only five hundred bushels of wheat and nine hundred bushels of potatoes were salvaged to feed a population of six hundred and seventy-three. But mushrooms, thriving in the piles of rotting tree bark where logs for the first homes had been taken, were found to help stave off starvation. Bushels of mushrooms were harvested there every morning for weeks at a time. They were light enough for a child to carry, so it was a common sight to see Ellis and the other children carrying large sacks full of mushrooms home on their backs.

Ellis remembered well these early sufferings. She was an introspective, sensitive child, with something of a poetic nature and a high intellectual capacity.

> Those first winters in Utah, notwithstanding the heroic efforts of preparation, were indeed very bleak and cold and trying. The wheat crop must have been scanty, as I well remember our many meals of corn bread and homemade beet sugar, with an occasional small slice of bacon. Butter was a rare treat in those struggling years, as was white bread.
>
> I well remember my dear father carrying home from the mill in a small white sack a few handfuls of wheat flour, the toll of all the wheat he had ground that day. This was carefully conserved for my beloved grandmother who was growing old and at that time in ill health with failing appetite. How carefully my beloved mother would prepare lovely-looking "short cakes" as they were then called. Not even a child thought of crying for them, for they were for dear, dear grandmother whom we so loved and hoped and prayed would be well again.
>
> I wonder now if anyone who watched me clearing up her tray noticed that I picked up every tiny crumb of that delicious bread. Never to this day has the best bread or cake tasted so good. Now even after almost a century has passed I seem to taste it yet, and how glad I am that, child as I was, I did not cry for a piece! Was this, I wonder, the beginning of self-abnegation, a self-denial and sacrifice of what I loved best, that lesson I seemed predestined to learn to its ultimate degree.[14]

There were, in spite of hard times, moments of pleasure, celebrations where the people gathered with glad hearts, forgetting their troubles and counting their blessings. There may have been nothing but fried doughnut dolls in the Christmas stockings, but there were sled rides in the frozen winter, spelling bees, quilting parties, swings and teeter-totters built for the children to play on, horseback riding, picnics at the lake and canyons, and the wonderful Fourth and Twenty-fourth of July celebrations.

Ellis wrote of these days: "My father and mother were the artists who created the flags and banners — the most marvelous to me to be hoisted on the very tall pole at sunrise with the salute of ten cannon peals, the smaller flags and banners with their inscriptions to be carried in the parade."[15]

The parade, for a small town in the 1850s, was impressive. The martial band rode in a carriage drawn by four gray horses. Next came the Mormon Battalion, then twenty-four young men in uniform followed by twenty-four young girls dressed all in white, twenty-four boys with flags, and twenty-four younger girls bearing the motto, Our Children — Our Glory. Following the parade, the people gathered to hear the orators of the day, then followed toasts, refreshments, and dancing until midnight. Ellis, young, spirited, and romantic, entered in with her whole heart.

> How early I rose this morning, elated with the thought that I, too, was a unit in the marching band, clothed in my best white gown beside my best and dearest friend Lydia Staker in her white dress. For years as the nation's natal day came round we two had this what then seemed to us a very great honor. I remember even yet how we would talk it over in our bed out-of-doors, between our times of watching the stars, the "dipper", "the seven sisters,"and other constellations. . . .[16]

In order to understand Ellis as a woman — her self-discipline, her drive, her inner pride — it is necessary to gain some insight into the life and character of her mother and the tenacious bond existing between the two.

From the earliest days Ellis worshipped her gentle mother, who was really only a girl when Ellis was born. And as she grew to womanhood and had her own children, her mother became the pattern for all she did, the standard against which she measured her own efforts, struggling to not fall short of the shining goal.

Anna Reynolds was not a strong and robust woman, but she knew her duty and performed her role as wife and mother with dignity and fortitude. Ellis called her "spiritually pure and strong," gentle in her manners, kind with others, never one to gossip or judge. The oft-repeated advice she gave her daughter rings of practicality: "If you cannot speak well of another, say nothing."[17] She was used to the quiet heroics of self-sacrifice, and endeared herself to others by her service. And, above all other things, she taught Ellis how to work.

> My dear mother, a prototype, awake and alert — each morning found her with a smiling face and willing hands caring for her household, her plans all made beforehand, her precious time budgeted for each meal to be prepared, the number of skeins of yarn she would spin, the stockings she would darn, the buttons to sew on, the clothing to be mended, her hours for the garden, wash days, soap-making days, candles to be moulded, times for dyeing her skeins, even her bread-making and dishwashing all scheduled so that when the frugal evening meal was over and every performance cleared up, she was ready for the rest and joy of the beautiful evening hour. Then, while her husband read to her or the two conversed, she with still-busy fingers created pretty laces to adorn her children's clothing, to decorate her household furnishings, curtains and valances, table cloths and pillow slips . . . for indeed in those days those skillful hands were never found idle in her waking hours. . . .[18]

One time an elderly neighbor appeared at their door unexpectedly, very late in the evening hours. Anna was confused as to the purpose of her visit until the sister, with a twinkle in her kind eyes confided, "Well, I thought I would just slip in at this late hour and see if for once I could find you without work in your hands. But I will not try again, Anna, for now I know."[19]

Anna added little personal touches to her homemaking, and demonstrated ingenuity as well as skill. In the early days when materials were unavailable she made the tops of the children's shoes from cloth, tipping the toes and heels with leather from the best of the worn-out shoes, backstitching it on with strong thread. Once when Ellis was in desperate need of a warm dress for school, Anna took one of her homespun woolen blankets, dyed it a soft black, and made a comfortable well-fitting dress for her daughter. It was often said of her by her neighbors that Anna Reynolds could cook the best meal out of nothing of anyone in the world.

Ellis threw herself, with her usual commitment and enthusiasm, into learning all of her mother's skills, even the difficult, distasteful things. Many were the pans of soda she gathered, used by her mother in making both soap and biscuits. She learned how to assist with the soap- and candle-making, helping her mother place a wick in each long tube and then pour the hot melted tallow inside. She called this "an unpleasant task," yet she willingly did it, as well as boiling the big kettles on soap-making day, kettles containing a fascinating assortment of left-over grease and oil, pork rind, wood ash, even meat bone to boil down together.

Anna was an excellent seamstress and taught her daughter how to wash the wool from the lambs, how to pick and card it into rolls, and then spin these into yarn, doubled and twisted and ready for knitting. A portion they would dye and then spin into finer yarn for weaving into cloth when they had their turn on the one loom in the village.

"The tailoring was all by my heroic mother," Ellis recorded, "making all of her children's and husband's clothing with the common needle, and so expert was she that she made many suits for those not of her family — stitching, stitching afar into the night."[20] This skill which she passed on to Ellis became a lifesaving blessing much later in her life.

One example of Ellis's desire to serve and do her part occurred at harvest time when she joined the group of gleaners who covered the fields after the harvesters had garnered the bulk of the crop. With a flail — a long, round stick — she walked the rows, picking up the few remaining stems of wheat heads, thrashing them on heavy canvas to separate the grain and chaff. After many days of such difficult work her young back ached, her head throbbed, her small hands were scratched and bleeding, her feet and ankles also scratched. But she had saved the precious grain and produced a whole bushel! And her bushel of wheat sold for fifteen dollars, a small fortune to turn over to the family cause.

The intensity of Ellis's nature, of her inner feelings, is portrayed in one brief line: "I had such a desire to do or try to do all the wonderful things my mother did!"[21]

It is fascinating to sit back and try to picture the routine that existed in this little pioneer home. Anna gave her daughter a gift as valuable as an ability to work hard; she bequeathed her a love of nature and beautiful things. Each Saturday they would polish the new glass windows, rubbing the precious stuff till it sparkled and shone. With soft homemade soap they would scour the chairs and tables, the long pine boards of the floor, even the woodwork, because as yet they had no paint. In summertime they would whitewash the huge fireplace, not used in the heat, then run to bathe in the cool lake waters, only pulling out the large wash tub if they ran out of time. But there was always time for the last task of the day, and this was Ellis's special domain.

She would race out into the fields and pick armfuls of flowers, the fragrant wild roses that were her mother's delight. Back home she would arrange them carefully in a stone jar of fresh water and place them before the clean, white fireplace. "What fragrance and what exquisite beauty as the tiny pretty buds opened day by day into those lovely pink blossoms so refreshing in their fragrance and beauty."[22] There was delight in Ellis's words which can be felt even now.

All her life Ellis had a thirst for knowledge. Books were a rare and cherished luxury. Education was very difficult to come by. Quills were used for pens, slate slabs in place of paper. Slate pencils were whittled from rock found in a hill near the mouth of Battle Creek Canyon. If ink was to be had it was made from oak bark boiled with copperas.

Possession of her first little McGuffy Reader was to Ellis a treasure. She loved to turn its pages over and over, feasting on the pictures as well as the words. Her desire for beauty was bound up with her hunger for knowledge.

> The few primitive pictures I had chanced to see whetted my desire for more—"The Boys Purloining the Farmer's Apples" and "The Country Maid Tossing her Vain Head with her Milk Pail Surmounting It." These pictures, with just a few others—all I could enjoy outside of those nature had painted.[23]

Her store of books was extremely limited. She had the McGuffy Readers and Webster's spelling book and somehow, from somewhere, an old dictionary. These were pored over in every minute she could find to spare from working. Her dictionary, in fact, was her constant companion. She purposefully sewed the large pockets in her dresses even larger to accommodate its bulk, and when she could find a lull from sewing or dishwashing, out would come the book. She was so starved for reading that she would go over the pages of dull definitions word by word.

With discernment, with instinct beyond her years, Ellis "seemed intuitively to know there were better things somewhere in this world for children."[24]

Ellis was a sensitive girl and she struggled with many childish uncertainties and fears. One of the greatest of these was a terror of being punished by the teacher. She was particularly zealous in her efforts to avoid being late, and would run screaming down the street if she considered herself in danger of being tardy. She was rewarded for her efforts by escaping the dreaded punishment. But once, through misadventure, punishment came, and the shame and injustice remained with her all her life. Ironically, it was her love of beauty that initiated her unwarranted pain.

> With a number of other girls I was sitting on a high rough slab bench next to my cousin, Susan. Our feet couldn't touch the floor and there was no back to lean upon. That morning I had gathered a few wild rose petals as I passed a bush in full bloom and slipped them in my book—I loved them so. When I opened my book my cousin spied them, and blew them mischievously. Instinctively I jumped to catch them—all this without a word, for we were punished for whispering. Unfortunately for me, the teacher happened to glance that way at the moment I was off my seat and I was marched to the end of the room and made to stand up the whole afternoon before all my schoolmates. Oh, the humiliation! All those hours I stood with noiseless sobs, and covered face, my apron soaked with tears. I can see the checks of pink and white in that apron to this day.
>
> As the children passed out at the close of school the teacher told me I could get down, and when I dared remove the wet covering of my face I saw a true friend, my little uncle Jimmie, just a few years my senior. Tears were in his eyes and with an arm around me he took me home. As we walked along I said to him, "Oh, please don't tell mother." When he said, "Don't cry and I will not tell anybody," how I loved him and appreciated his tender sympathy. He was so loving and kind, and sensitive, and had never before in his life seen me punished. I had ever been the treasured one of our household.[25]

The shame of punishment, of disappointing her beloved mother, was greater than her need for comfort which, at least in part, Jimmie was able to provide.

With the years she grew in self-confidence and her inner power — her sense of values, her dignity — began to make themselves manifest in her person and her actions. By the time she was fourteen years old she had attained a position of respect with the teacher — a different one from that of her earliest years. She had begun to act as a teaching assistant, helping the primary classes. This brought her great pleasure. Yet she did not hesitate to risk this satisfaction and prestige when a time of decision came.

One day the teacher began to punish a young boy, as Ellis says, "cruelly." The boy's older brother was moved to come to his assistance, which brought the teacher's wrath down upon him. Ellis watched for as long as she could bear it. In all her life she had never seen such cruelty. At last she threw back her head and stepped forward, planting herself in the very center of the room. She was weeping, but her voice when she spoke held strength and firmness.

"Mr. A., you quit that this moment," she said.

Instantly the teacher stopped; his arm fell. He stood in the silent room. Ellis held her breath. "I will stop for this girl's sake," the man responded. "But I would not stop for anyone else."

How grateful she was then for her courage! "I am thankful to this day," she recorded, "for the God-given power to check cruelty and injustice."[26]

In spite of all this Ellis was able to state: "My early school life, crude as it was, was a joy to me."[27] And her parents were not insensitive to her needs or her feelings. Often she heard them state their desire to give their children an education, to make sure they missed not one opportunity. During one particularly severe, snow-bound winter, they were forced to remain in the canyon and work at the mill. Yet they gave permission for Ellis to stay in the valley, cared for by her grandparents, so she would be able to go to school.

This separation from her parents and brothers and sisters was hard for the sensitive Ellis to bear. Yet, kindly, it was a form of preparation for the final separation when it came. Occasionally she

was taken up for visits, riding in the covered phaeton her grandparents owned. She spoke of the unbounded joy of those reunions,
the loving embraces and tender words. And, hand in hand, she tells
of the beauty. Never were her discerning eye and tender spirit
untouched by the simple day-to-day beauties.

> The rushing of the waters through the mill, the rumbling of its
> machinery, the icy banks of the dashing streams, the frozen spray
> on bush and trees, the little log cabin covered with snow on the
> nearby hillside and towering mountains on every hand, seemed so
> wonderful — almost more than a reality.[28]

So the youthful years passed for Ellis, colored by her own
passion and poetry.

2

Death and Discovery

Ellis, as she began to grow out of childhood, developed a lovely carriage and a fascinating face. She had a fine slender nose, a warm, sensitive mouth, fair clear skin and high cheekbones, and a wealth of brown hair that shone darkly against her white skin. But her most arresting feature was her eyes: large, deep-set, dark and piercing, glowing with spirit, intelligence, and innocent wonder.

Offers for marriage came before she had reached her teens. One of these she happened to hear her parents discussing; the brother of her nearest friend had asked for her hand! She was shocked. She was still just a child—she still played with her dolls! Thoughts of boys and romance were far from her mind. Her parents' reaction was similar to her own, and she breathed in relief. But the short days narrowed. Life was coming around the corner a little too quickly.

One of Ellis's dearest friends was the widow Lydia Mayhew, whom she called simply "Aunt Liddy." Aunt Liddy's daughter, "Cal," was near Ellis's age, and the widow welcomed the crowd of girls to her home, where they spent many entertaining hours. One day in July of 1859, the summer after Ellis's twelfth birthday, she ran into Aunt Liddy's house on a simple errand and was invited to sit down and join the family, who were poring delightedly over some family photos. What entertainment! Ellis joined in eagerly, exclaiming about each dear one, asking questions. These were the faces of friends and relatives left back east when the family emigrated to Utah. Ellis looked at dozens of uncles, aunts, and cousins, then opened up a daguerreotype enclosed in a small black case.

Silently she gazed at the features; the "most interesting, truly handsome face"[1] she had ever seen. The eyes were fascinating; they seemed to pierce right through her. It was as though she were lost in a spell that the face had created. "How wonderful," she cried, to the others' amazement. "This is the man I am going to marry!"[2]

Her words, as she said herself, were "spontaneous and unpremeditated," and came from a serious, thrilling sensation she felt deep inside. It was no girlish joke she uttered. But Cal's ringing laughter answered her mockingly.

"Oh, Ellis, I'm going to tell him. Just as soon as he comes," her friend taunted.

"What do you mean?" Ellis felt her heart pounding. "Is it possible I will see him?"

"Oh, yes, to be sure. The company of Saints arrives here tomorrow, and my cousin will be with them. He's joined the Church and has come to locate his family in Utah."[3]

Ellis struggled now with conflicting emotions: She longed to meet Milford Shipp face to face. But she was sensitive, naturally modest by nature; she was only twelve years old and shy. She couldn't bear to have her words repeated for everyone to laugh at — especially him!

But he arrived the following day; nothing could stop that. She stood by her friend and watched the joyful reunion and thought her own thoughts.

> After three months of travel by ox team and no barber! One might try to describe his appearance, but it was my opinion no artist could ever do him justice! He had the manner, attitude, and dignity of a prince.
>
> He was bronzed, tanned from long exposure to summer suns and mountain breezes. His eyes were the most wonderful I had ever beheld, and so was his jet black hair. I knew he was a cultured gen-

tleman and I feared he would consider us all rude, unladylike country girls. . . .[4]

How painfully aware she was of her lack of age and attain-
ments! She suppressed her smiles in her kerchief and tried not to
giggle. Milford Shipp was very polished and very witty. Strangers,
especially tall, handsome strangers, were rare in their quiet community. With honest enthusiasm they showed him welcome, with
a round of entertainments in his honor.

At the first party, the night of his arrival, the honored guest
danced only twice. He was tired from his long travels. But he
danced with his cousin, Cal, and with her good friend Ellis, whose
beseeching looks must have moved her friend into "not telling," so
she was not shamed by the feelings she had revealed.

The next few weeks were an awakening for Ellis. There were
outings during the day and dinners and parties in the evening. Her
own mother invited the Mayhews and their guest to dinner. Ellis
remembered that he complimented the biscuits, asking, "Did Ellis
make them?" And she blushed because she could not take the
honor, and because he had thought of her and singled her out.

Milford Shipp was eleven years Ellis's senior, having been
born in 1836. He was graduated from Wabash College in Indiana: a
man of experience, from a wealthy family. Yet here, in this setting,
the two were thrown together. At the social gatherings she found
herself seated beside him. She would listen to him almost rever-
ently, impressed by his voice, his smile, his spontaneous kindness,
his views about the gospel and serious things. And, although they
were simple and homey, their evenings together were more romantic in nature than Ellis knew.

Dancing by candlelight, singing around sagebrush fires the
melodious strains of "Annie Laurie" and "Nellie Gray," Milford
couldn't help being impressed by the girl beside him as she half-
closed her beautiful eyes and dreamed, while the gentle strains of
the music floated about them. But she was only a child, although
she seemed much older. He reminded himself of this fact dozens of
times.

One fine afternoon the group of young people, which consisted of Cal and his two brothers, Cal's cousin Alonzo Farns-

worth, Lydia Stoker, Susan MacArthur, Ellis, and "Milf," rode out to the lovely lake four miles distant. They wandered along the shore together, laughing and talking and gathering shells. It was considered good luck to find a stone with a hole clear through it. Milf found one and gave it to Ellis to keep. She did—she kept it the rest of her life, through times of good luck and times of shadow and sorrow.

He became a part of her life. The autumn and winter passed for her in one round of pleasure. It was the only innocent, carefree time Ellis was to know before sorrow would lay a permanent hand on her heart. She saw deeply into the man, even at her young age. And he awakened in her much more than romantic notions.

> His ideas of progression and life's possibilities were an inspiration, a vital spark igniting my latent mental fires of determination to study, to improve in every phase of life, to be something, an identity; at least to have an ideal and work to that end. As a magnet draws another object near, thus did his personality attract mine.[5]

With spring came a blow to her happiness; Milford was leaving, returning to his home in the east. A chance reading of Parley P. Pratt's "Voice of Warning" had converted him and brought him the thousands of miles to the gathering place of the Mormon people. Here he had been baptized in October 1857; he then returned to Missouri to act as guide for immigrant trains coming to Utah. He had in mind finding a place where his parents could settle. He was going back now to teach them the truths he had learned.

His departure engendered all kinds of alarming emotions. Ellis wondered if, when he got back to his home, he would forget both her and his new religion and she would never see him again. "I presume it is needless to say," she wrote, "that I was as deeply in love as girls of that age for the first time can love."[6]

Their last afternoon together the young people took a carriage ride up American Fork Canyon as far as they could go, then stopped and walked the rough, narrow trails. Milford and Austin took a short trip up into the hills and came back with wildflowers, bunches of early spring violets. Milford handed her the fragrant blossoms. "Here's a bouquet for Ellis," he said.[7] She remembered the afternoon as one of pure pleasure.

The evening was to be a grand finale to the day; they had planned to spend it together at Aunt Lydia's house. But her mother, much to Ellis's consternation, forbade her going out again. She pleaded, but in vain; her mother had spoken and her word was law.

Perhaps Anna sensed that her daughter's emotions were running too deeply; perhaps she wanted to avoid possible danger ahead. Whatever the cause, this last pleasure was snatched and in a sudden destroyed. They had parted at the gate with the expectation of meeting again in a few brief hours. Neither dreamed the many scenes they should pass through before time would bring them together again.

Another romantic episode took place about this same time in Ellis's life, one of those strange, inexplicable circumstances which come unbidden, and mark and change us against our will. In 1860 when Ellis was just thirteen, a young man named William Daniels came to Pleasant Grove. He was a new convert to the Church, described as one of sterling integrity, pleasant, intelligent, honest, and industrious. He, too, was many years Ellis's senior. Yet he seemed to fall in love with her at first sight.

He became instantly devoted and attentive, and his attentions couldn't help but be flattering. With her sensitive heart Ellis appreciated his "nobility of character" and respected him. But she was not able to return the ardent nature of his love. Her parents, her mother in particular, were concerned, especially when the young man succeeded in pressuring Ellis, after many anguished entreaties, to promise to become his wife as soon as she reached a suitable age. He boarded at her home for a while and Ellis began to resent his advances, to feel trapped by his intense emotions, his claims upon her. She was determined to find a way out of her commitment, and at last an opportunity came.

One evening she was sitting alone with Lydia when Will walked into the room. Half-teasingly he announced he was going to kiss her. Instantly her hot pride flared up. How dare he be so free with another present! She spoke sharply to him but he persisted. She warned him that if he made any further advances she would slap his face—an unladylike thing, but she felt driven to it. William ignored the warning and continued to importune her. Ellis kept her word and slapped him across the cheek.

This was considered a very serious insult. He resented it, though he did not berate her in words. However, a coolness grew between them. For weeks they scarcely exchanged a word. And it was the means of breaking their engagement, to everyone's relief but Will's. Ellis admitted that she did all in her power to make him dislike her. But nothing could move his affections for her. Ellis felt, even after years had passed, that "he, of all men, loved me most,"[8] and was aware of the unbounded nature of his devotion.

About this time Anna Reynolds became seriously ill. For years Anna's health had been failing, so she had gradually trained Ellis to take over more and more of the household responsibilities. Now her time was very short, though they didn't know it. But the sweet influence of her spirit still reigned in her home and a gentle family unity prevailed there. William Reynolds was devoted to Anna. One incident beautifully bears out this fact.

Anna's sickbed was so situated that she could gaze out of the little east window to the green slopes of the towering mountains whose far, ragged peaks were still laced with snow. Her own body was burning hot, consumed with fever. "Oh, for a ball of that snow," she cried.[9]

The following morning, very early, William was missing. The rest of the household went about their chores. But the hours passed without their father returning. Grandmother Hawley came to sit with her daughter. Where was William? At last, in the late afternoon, he walked into the yard carrying a small tin pail, carefully covered. Inside, wrapped in thick sacks, were hard-packed snowballs he had formed and cared for carefully. He had walked the long, hard miles to the distant snow line and was back now with his offering; something to cool the brow of his sweetheart, to bring a smile back into her beautiful blue eyes.

During her mother's illness Ellis's suitor, Will Daniels, performed every kindness he could think of to ease her load, though inadvertently he made things harder for her, adding to the burden of frustrated guilt Ellis carried concerning him.

Ellis turned fourteen years old January 20, 1861. On January 27 her mother drifted into a coma, remaining in this state for hours. Then suddenly she opened her eyes, "so like the blue of sky." "I am not going now," she announced in a clear strong voice. "I have so much to tell you." The blue eyes shone. "I have been to a heavenly sphere—I have seen such glorious things."[10]

Anna was eager to share with her loved ones what she had experienced, but they were fearful, worried that any exertion might cause her to slip away from them once again. Gently they hushed her. "Gain back your strength," they told her. "There'll be plenty of time to tell us then." She was so desirous; she tried time and again. But no one wanted the responsibility of listening, of endangering her fragile existence. She would get well. She could tell them of her heavenly visit then. And so the beautiful tale was never spoken, the glorious secrets went with her into her grave.

During the next day she called each loved one to her, giving them final instructions, expressing her love. Above all she besought them to remain faithful and true to the gospel and to serve their Heavenly Father all their lives. George and James were active, growing schoolboys. Theirs would be the task of helping and working with their father. The little girls, Anna and Sarah, were too young to help much, too young to understand. So to Ellis was left the burden of Anna's instruction.

First she secured a promise important to her: Ellis was not to marry William Daniels; Ellis gave her word. Then, with her sweet voice trembling and earnest, Anna begged Ellis to care for her precious little ones, to be an example, a teacher, a mother in her absence, a help to her father, a comfort to Anna's parents. The words and their import sunk deep into Ellis's soul. There was one last press of the loving fingers against her hand, then nothing but the awesome and total loss.

"Oh, how could she go?" Ellis cried. "Surrounded by so many hearts that held her as their most priceless treasure?"[11]

She was sustained, even at her young age, by her faith in the gospel, her surety that her mother was happy and well. She believed that the Eternal Father had called her mother, and she had been taught not to question His will. She loved the truths her mother had lived and died for. She would do her best to live up to them now.

But still there were the times of darkness and anguish. She felt deeply the loss of her mother's love, which she called "so like unto God's love." There were still the terrible, lonely hours when she lay crying, wondering what to do, and how to find the strength to go on.

One of the greatest things to sustain her was force of example, the precious legacy her parents had given her. She could not remember hearing a cross word pass between them. They held out to her gaze an image of ideal love, an image she worked toward for the rest of her life, a standard she would fiercely hold onto and never abandon.

> My home was a blessed sanctuary of love and peace. Perhaps it was too much a heaven for this mortal probation and could not continue forever. Peace, unity of purpose, faith, true Christian charity to each other, the uplift of culture and refinement—purity, honor, virtue, honesty our standard. All words spoke love and interest in the other's welfare. Anything short of this could never have filled my ideal of a wedded life. God bless them for this example to me, their child! My soul thrills with gratitude to them, and to the Great Giver of all such blessings.[12]

Another thing that kept Ellis going was her father's need. She was aware how great was the gap in his life now. "The early passing of my beloved mother in her thirty-first year seemed to break the sacred circle of our domestic life, for when an entity is cut in twain the one half can stand securely only through the uplift of divine power."[13]

Anna's younger half-sister, Sarah Ellis, wrote: "There never was anyone else whom William adored like he did Anna."[14] Ellis tried to fill her mother's place in his life, yet at the same time appreciated all he did for her; it was surely a matter of the two going forth into the darkness hand in hand. He set an example by gently serving her and the others, by being man enough to express his own tender sympathies.

But the task Ellis set for herself was awesome.

> I, the eldest, knew best and remembered more of her wise, loving tenderness, her ambitions for our education, our need to learn

the joys of work, never to sit down and let others do for us what we could do for ourselves. She taught us to be clean in body, mind, and soul, to be obedient, respectful, and reverent to our elders, to be chaste in thought and word and deed, never to tell an unclean or vulgar story and never to listen to one. No wonder that I, the eldest, must needs experience an early transition from young girlhood to womanhood.[15]

William Daniels, though apparently rejected, gave of his strength to Ellis at this difficult time, anticipating her needs, her very desires. "Oh, how every kind word and look smote my heart," Ellis wrote, "for I knew I must not encourage them. I did not love him, but oft my heart would warm with pity when he made his appeals for a place in my affections."[16]

Anna's parents gave of their strength to Ellis—as they always had, as they always would. "I can never forget the wise loving watch-care of my aging grandparents, their sweet sympathetic advice, the comfort of being near them, realizing every day the strength and uplift of their tender love, wisdom and example."[17]

In the summer Will Daniels's health began to fail. He turned to Ellis's grandparents in his need. They took him into their home and cared for him like a son through months of illness. Ellis lived in an agony of self-reproach. It was a situation too adult in its implications for her to handle, especially on top of all she was coping with in regard to her mother's death. By late autumn his condition had become severe. Ellis pleaded in her prayers that his life might be spared. She felt undertones among their mutual friends that responsibility for his death would be laid at her door.

One evening Ellis entered his room, after having been several days absent. He gazed into her face intently, with a look that sent shudders along her frame. One of his watchers asked, "Do you know who this is?"

"Yes," he replied, "it is my wife."[18]

Ellis turned and fled to regain her composure. These were the last coherent words she heard him utter. William Daniels died a few days later.

Ellis was thrown into a period of guilty self-reproach, dwelling upon the pain she had caused him "whose greatest fault was in loving one too well."[19] There were many tears, much inner anguish. How she longed for the comforting influence of her mother, the gentle wisdom she'd always relied upon. She recorded in her journal:

> After this I became sorrowful and moody, no more the gay, lighthearted girl I had ever been. I still went into society, but I did not join in the sports with my wonted alacrity, for every pleasure was fraught with a degree of sadness.[20]

In addition to the pressures of caring for her younger brothers and sisters and running the household, there was the ever-present problem of insufficient funds. Ellis longed to ease her father's heavy burden, but felt frustrated by the narrow possibilities before her. Whenever she could she "worked out," earning usually not more than a pittance, but happy to be doing whatever she could.

One year she worked all through the summer and earned a single print gown for her efforts. It was a trial for Ellis's proud spirit to be looked upon as "servant status." One family who regarded her in this manner went far enough to abuse her sensitive spirit. She cried out her complaints to her grandmother. Ellis Hawley immediately bristled into action. Uncle Asa was sent to the house to collect Ellis's trunk, soon returning with it hefted high on his shoulder.

"You blessed child," he told Ellis, "you never need go there again."[21]

But it seemed Ellis was to have no respite. That same summer while attending a party, her friend Cal told Ellis the news she had just received: Milford Bard Shipp had married a young heiress. The lady was both beautiful and educated, and Milf had apparently loved her from childhood. This was a devastating, though subtle, form of rejection. "My last hope," Ellis recorded, "was gone."[22]

About this same time her father brought a new wife into the household. Perhaps at a later time Ellis could have borne it; perhaps if one or two of her pressing sorrows had been lifted. But to have another woman take her place when she had been fiercely proud of "doing" for her father—to have this woman step into her mother's role, preside in her place at dinner, use her things, sit in the easy chair her mother sat in—even be called by her mother's name: Christina Larsen actually had two given names, one of them coincidentally "Anna."

Later, of course, the perspective came. Ellis was able to write of her stepmother:

> One not strong physically, but a noble, kind woman, with gentle, lovable nature and true motherly instincts. I, and all my mother's children, have ever loved and honored her — our dear Aunt Christina.[23]

But at the time her advent broke Ellis's young heart. She spoke much of the struggling to control her jealous feelings, of being forced to learn unselfishness very young. Yet she admits that Christina was a true mother to the younger children and that the household was still basically one of harmony and peace.

But Ellis was too old to become one of Christina's children. The role she had so painfully created, the niche she had made for herself, had now been usurped. From this point on, for the next few years, Ellis struggled with the sensation that she had no home, no place where she truly belonged.

One unlooked-for advantage came with Christina's arrival. Ellis was freed from the responsibility of running her father's house. During the following winter, 1862-63, she went to visit her friend, Lide Hybette, in the city. It was her first visit of any consequence and she admits that to her the marvels of Salt Lake City seemed as wildly exciting as the wonders of Rome.

For the first time Ellis attended the theatre, seeing Ora Lyne in the play "Damon and Pythias," which was probably staged in the Social Hall; the new theatre was just nearing completion. She also attended a dance held at Social Hall. She was accustomed to rough floors — and rougher manners — tallow candles, and one violin. Here were brilliant lights, soft gentle music, guests with dress and manners as refined as their surroundings. She was fascinated by the smooth, springy floor and by Truman Angell's bust of Shakespeare which brooded over the graceful arch that curved above the stage.

At this party she met a young man named Zebulon Jacobs. He was very attentive and lavish in his flattery. This was only a chance encounter, but a few evenings later Ellis attended a ball and met him again. He spoke his praises of her to others and this also pleased her. Besides, Zebulon was a stepson of Brigham Young's, and son of one of the prophet's most prominent wives, Zina D. Huntington. This rendered his advances more memorable than they may otherwise have been.

Lide urged her friend to stay the winter and Ellis delightedly agreed, assisting Lide's aunt, Clarissa Robison, with her sewing. But some four or five weeks later her father sent word that he would be moving to Sanpete as soon as he could complete arrangements. He had been asked to go and settle this new, barren region. Ellis thought it was almost an imposition. "Just as they were beginning to see the light of a new dawning in their home," she said, "when the flour bin was not so often empty, when they could reasonably believe their most trying days were at an end. Then to start it all over again!"[24]

Ellis made her own very difficult decision. She would not go with her father when he left Battle Creek. There were things she wanted in life, and Sanpete didn't have them. But she returned to spend as much time with her family as she could before their departure.

The farewell was more difficult than she had expected. Her brothers and sisters were more than just that to her: she had mothered them; they were bound together with promises, with that line of love and birth that stretched now to the grave. And it was hard to see the old house left empty and quiet. Here they had spent so many happy days, here they had banded together in sorrow, here moved the shadows of Anna's voice and face.

At this time her father had two wives, both converts from Scandinavia. He left the younger at Pleasant Grove with Ellis and for two months they kept house in the empty rooms. But both were young and very lonely and spent most of their hours at Grandma Hawley's being mothered by her.

On the third of May, Ellis returned to the city, staying with Sister Robison. It was peaceful here; there was time for some quiet reflection. Not until the end of June did her life pick up. Then, while visiting one of her new friends, Belle Whitney, she chanced to meet Zebulon Jacobs again. His gallantry, his interest had not diminished. There was a ball held the third of July and he was there. Even though Ellis came with a partner, Charles Alby, Mr. Jacobs allowed his preference for her to be known.

But the end of July saw Ellis back in Pleasant Grove, staying with either her Uncle Asa or Grandpa Hawley. She couldn't shake the loneliness of her spirit, the vague discontent that hovered around her mind. Nor could she turn her back on her awareness that, though she had places to go, she had no real home.

Four years had passed since Milford Shipp left Utah. The years had not been kind to him. Soon after his first son was born he was called on a mission to England. His wife, Cornelia Winn, had not been converted to the gospel. It was difficult for her to understand how he could turn his back on wife and child and go halfway around the world for religion's sake. Her friends began to prejudice her against him. By the time he returned in April, Nellie had left him and demanded a bill of divorcement on grounds of religion.

But Milford had been called back from his mission early for an express purpose, to assist his parents to immigate to Zion. His mother staunchly believed, but not his father, who harbored some resentments against the Church. But he agreed to the move west because of the conditions and circumstances of the Civil War. He felt Utah would be totally removed from any danger or conflict — and it was.

The fact that the Civil War was raging meant little to the struggling pioneers. They were too far away to be drawn into the drama and pathos; there was struggle and tragedy enough in their own lives. Ellis in her history never gives it mention except this once, in regard to Milford's parents.

In the autumn of 1863 Milford arrived in Battle Creek. Ellis, now sixteen — far removed from twelve — but young, feeling young and shy still, walked the familiar path to Cal's house, her emotions churning. Before she reached the house she could hear his voice. It startled her how familiar the tones could sound. She believed she had weaned her feelings entirely from him. But this first evening proved otherwise. "I soon learned," she recorded, "that his powers of fascination had lost none of their enchantment."[25]

He accompanied her home. There was a "marked kindness" in his manner toward her. And yet, after his trips to the city came back the rumors that he was paying attentions to a Miss Eldrege there. Ellis was torn. Had he discovered her feelings, and was he merely toying with them?

It may have seemed so to her the evening when Milf, who had just returned from one of his visits to the city, attended their peach-paring party. Lon, his young cousin, had been filling Ellis's ears with stories of Milford's devotion to Miss Eldrege. When she entered the room Milf was sitting by a large basket of peaches. There was an empty seat beside him. "Sit here," he said.

But at the same time Cal cried from across the room, "No, come sit by me." She crossed and sat by her friend, perhaps secretly wanting to see if he would pursue her, would press the point. He did not. He had a quick pride that could match her own. When Lydia entered the room he called out to her, "Here comes my girl!"[26] He spent the whole evening with her, laughing and talking, ignoring Ellis, who was miserable, more than justly punished. Their relationship, their early courtship, seemed destined to such ups and downs.

About this time Brigham Young called Milford Shipp, along with George A. Smith and Franklin D. Richards to serve as a "home missionary" to travel up and down the scattered settlements "teaching and encouraging the Saints."[27] In one trip alone they held thirty-eight meetings, and this in the month of February when conditions of travel must have been very trying.

Milford was a natural, gifted speaker. He was in many ways a romantic at heart. Even his education reflected this. His course of study at the university concentrated on Greek and Latin, Plutarch, history, and philosophy. In his freshman year he had roomed with Lew Wallace, who was later to write the novel *Ben Hur*. He was more wont to grow excited about "air castles" than down-to-earth practicalities. And yet, his belief in the gospel was deeply rooted. It had already come through a fiery trial or two. He could expound the principles with power and persuasion, combining his artistic gifts with the intellectual strength of his convictions.

When Ellis first heard him speak she was overcome. She had thought of him as romantic and charming, clever—the life of the party, the leader in fun. This insight into his powers was like a revelation to her. "As I listened I thought I had never before heard a man advance such pure and holy principles."[28] It was yet another hold he had taken upon her heart.

Ellis longed to be able to go to school that winter. But there was no school in Pleasant Grove and no money to pay for tuition in the city. Yet her friend, Belle, had been writing, urging her to come "and make her a good long visit."[29] So she went to the city anyway and stayed with Belle and her mother, wife of President Daniel H. Wells. They treated her with the greatest kindness.

While Ellis was there, on December 12, 1863, she received her endowments, the holy ordinances of the Lord's house. This was a momentous experience for her, and she was aware of its import, although she wasn't quite seventeen. "This occurrence caused me to think more deeply than I had ever done before regarding my religion, which I believe had a tendency to make me a better woman."[30]

Another important thing happened during this visit. Zebulon Jacobs proposed and Ellis accepted him. "I never heard any lover more ardent in professions of love and devotion than he was," she recalled. And yet she also recorded her own reaction. "Perhaps I was in love, but I think it was a powerful fascination that had its hold upon my senses."[31]

It was the holiday season in the city and Ellis was young. She had had too little of innocent laughter and pleasure. "I attended many balls and theatres," she confided, "and gave myself entirely to the intoxication of pleasure."[32]

The Christmas Eve ball was held in the Nineteenth Ward assembly room. Mr. Shipp was there with his sister, Flora . . . and Miss Eldrege. Ellis felt "a happy triumph" in the attentions of Mr. Jacobs. Why, then, did she feel such regret a few days later when, traveling to visit her father, she stopped at Salt Creek and, too tired to attend a meeting of traveling missionaries, missed hearing Milford Bard speak? Why was the loss like a pain inside her?

She chided herself. "He's just an old friend, that's all. He's going east this spring—good-bye!"[33] She herself was traveling south not just to visit, but to see for herself what her father's reaction would be, to gain his consent for her marriage to Zebulon Jacobs.

It was wonderful to be under her father's roof again, within the protecting family circle. But times were still very difficult for her father and while she was there she was called upon to witness a terrible suffering. One of her father's wives lost a little child, an infant daughter. Ellis suffered the loss of the small half sister herself, and felt deep sympathy for the intense suffering of the mother.

William Reynolds felt satisfied with Zebulon Jacobs's character from letters he had received from the young man and the reports Ellis now gave him. There seemed little more to consider. So in a few weeks Ellis returned to Pleasant Grove, to her grandmother, and attended the annual Church conference in Salt Lake City in April with her grandfather and his other wife, Sarah. Then she spent the remainder of the summer working for Grandmother Ellis in Battle Creek. Her grandmother paid her wages for doing housework. Mr. Jacobs was offended that she did not remain in the city. But Ellis knew she needed to somehow earn her way.

In late August she made a short trip there, but Zeb had gone east to assist immigration. She missed seeing Zina D. Young by just a few hours—Sister Young called round with her carriage shortly after Ellis had left to return home—so a few days later Ellis received a kind letter inviting her to visit Zina in her own home, not just for an afternoon, but for a few days "or as long as circumstances will permit." This, indeed, was a great honor and Zina underlined it by urging "do not feel any delicacy about letting me know or coming."[34]

Ellis was duly impressed, and duly touched. She called Zina "one of Zion's brightest stars" and even confided that she was "one I would like to fill my dear mother's place."[35] But this particular dream was not to materialize.

In October Ellis received a letter from Zebulon Jacobs breaking off the engagement, informing her that "the deep devotion he thought he had once entertained for her was but that of friendship."[36] Ellis was stunned. Heartbroken? Not really. She admitted that she "suffered a great wound to her maidenly pride."[37] She even toyed with the consideration that this might, perhaps, be punishment for past misdeeds.

To her great comfort her father was then in Pleasant Grove attending to business concerning his orchards and molasses mill. She told him she wanted to go home with him and he consented. But first he had business to conduct in the city, so Ellis accompanied him there. She happened to meet Milford while walking along the street. He urged her to call on his sister, which Ellis did. Flora said she had news to tell, but she would not tell it, rather insisted that she would write it in a letter when Ellis had returned home.

On November 1 she and her father returned to Pleasant Grove and she took a sad farewell of that loved place. On November 9 they started for Mount Pleasant. Ellis felt she was going among strangers and the old sense of loneliness crept back again.

But once there Ellis determined to use this time to improve herself. She often chided her own weakness, her own failure to "improve her time" and do all she could to learn and progress. Here in Mount Pleasant was a happy find, a young teacher by the name of Anthon Lund. He was a new arrival, a convert from Scandinavia, still going by the name "Antoine." He was well versed in a number of languages, a fine actor as well as a wonderful teacher. Ellis called him "one of the smartest men I ever knew." He taught school right there in her father's house and she attended, although she was definitely his oldest pupil. "The influence of his voice," she stated, "ever was inspiring to greater achievement. It seemed to me just what I had so long desired."[38]

Day-to-day life in Mount Pleasant was far from easy. Ellis told of one winter when her little brother arranged to milk a number of cows during the bitter cold weather in return for a pint of milk a day. His thin little body was insufficiently clad and he suffered from hunger, but he gallantly worked long hours for the luxury of fresh milk.

It would be well to remember here the praise of Christina which came from perhaps an unexpected source — Anna's little sister, Sarah Ellis, who in her parents' history said: "We all loved her and if there is a crown anywhere for anybody, Christina will get it, for she earned it because she walked faithfully and uncomplainingly her stony path to the end."[39]

Ellis suffered an awkward time or two herself. After she spent a happy afternoon with a number of girlfriends, one suggested that they draw straws to see whose house they should return to — which girl would treat them all to dinner. Ellis stiffened with dread. She knew the larder at home was practically empty. What would she do if the lot should fall to her? She would love to entertain them, but how could she do it? With all the fervor of girlish faith she prayed, and was spared the awful humiliation.

One morning Ellis slept late and her sister awoke her, telling her that a letter had arrived. This was nothing unusual; Ellis had many correspondents. She felt no strange sense of premonition. The letter was from Mrs. Ashton, an old acquaintance. It was long and newsy, but to Ellis's mind it may as well have contained but one sentence — a single sentence that burned into her mind: "Mr. Shipp and Miss Eldrege were married last week, November 19, 1864."[40] So this was the news Flora had to tell her! News she had been to afraid to speak face to face.

"Married again! Now I know he cares nothing for me. Oh well, I care nothing for him!" Such thoughts were Ellis's only defense now. But the news cast a bleakness over her days and ruined the mirth of the holiday season. "I think that time was the saddest of my life," she recorded.[41]

The future did indeed look bleak at this point. Even her intellectual awakening caused her pain. It served to whet her ambitions and desires. And yet, their fulfillment seemed so far away, so impossible without books or money, with "so much time consumed in gaining the common necessities of life, in just traveling from one place to another."[42]

Yet even in her sadness and suffering Ellis was always one to chide herself. "Why was I not happy?" she demanded of herself. "Why did I allow myself to indulge in regrets? I was at home then surrounded by my little brothers and sisters and under the protection of a kind and loving father. How blessed I was, but still I complained!"[43]

Ellis had always loved poetry. She was emotionally receptive to all it represented. During this period she memorized every poem she could discover in either a book or a current newspaper. Once committed to memory they were hers, something she could call forth in a moment of extreme pain or joy, when nothing else but poetry would do. Later in her life she was to publish a volume of her own poems. She wrote hundreds during her lifetime. So it seems natural to assume that now, in the depths of her inner turmoil and disappointment, she probably used verse to release and express her emotions.

In February the seesawing started again. The traveling missionaries arrived, Milford Shipp with them. It was customary then for managers in charge of the visitors' stay to arrange partners for the distinguished guests from among the local girls. Even if the men were married, it was considered gracious and proper to entertain them while they were there. Ellis and her cousin, Susan, had both been chosen as general partners, with no particular escort specified. Milford called on Ellis's family and during his visit asked Ellis to be his partner at the party which was to be given in the missionaries' honor the following night. She consented, thinking it would make no difference which of the missionaries she accompanied.

At the party all the young ladies chosen as partners sat in a special place on the stage. Brother Candland, floor manager, introduced them one by one to their companions. He began with Brother Franklin Richards. Ellis thought it was known she was to be Milford's partner. But to her surprise she heard Brother Candland politely introducing her to Brother Richards.

What was she to do? She didn't have enough quick presence of mind to frame a suitable excuse or explanation. She was forced to accept her partner graciously. "If Mr. Shipp will excuse me . . . " she stumbled.

"Certainly," came the reply in a tone so bitter that it cut into Ellis's already trembling heart. Poor Milford could never accept defeat and be gracious. He let Ellis know he considered her action a personal slight. Everyone seemed aware of the situation. His wife's father was there and, though it seems crude to our reckoning, he hugely enjoyed the joke on his son-in-law. Ellis did all she could to apologize, to atone for her very "grievous error." But Milford would not be placated; he gave no ground.

It is important to note this early pattern between them. Ellis, so naturally spirited and independent, accepted this almost haughty manipulation, this assumption that Milford was just in his expectations, no matter how extreme or demanding those expectations might be. He inspired her love, even adoration, he brought out her inner ambitions to rise, to improve. She seemed often content with that, and with that alone.

The missionaries left, Susan left, and Ellis was bereft and lonely again. She was eighteen and it seemed life was closing in upon her. At the end of the school quarter Mr. Lund took a vacation, so Ellis took a vacation as well and returned to Battle Creek and her grandparents. In April she and her friend Lydia went to Salt Lake to attend general conference. Her last day there, as fate would have it, they met Mr. Shipp while they were returning from church. Incredibly, he invited them to spend the evening with himself and his wife, asking that they bring his sister Flora with them.

They did so. Ellis had met Milford's wife only once before. She must have had mixed emotions concerning the evening, and what Mrs. Shipp's reception of them would be. They conversed for a while, then Flora entertained them, performing Smith's march "Floating on the Wind" as well as other pieces. Milford himself sang "A Little More Cider, Tom Moore," then asked his wife to play and sing for them. She did, but "a little reluctantly,"[44] Ellis observed. Ellis was certainly sensitive to the undercurrents she felt around her and prophesied to Lydia when they left that the marriage would end in separation. The presentiment was a strong one.

She returned to Battle Creek, then in May to Mount Pleasant, accompanied by her Uncle Asa and her cousin, Louisa Hawley.

The emotions of youth are always poignant. She remembered wandering the lakeshore where they had camped, in spots where the landscape was lonely and solitary. She and Louisa talked over their various misfortunes. Life had been very dismal for Ellis at times, dragging her through one tragedy after another, mocking her desires, holding her dearest dreams a tantalizing distance from her.

In Mount Pleasant she met her young cousin, Wesley, son of one of her father's brothers. He had come for a visit, though that seems surprising since his sentiments were assuredly anti-Mormon. But he was a decent boy with a kind heart and the two became good, though sometimes wary, friends.

On June 3 Susan Hawley lost her small son. This was even more tragic than the death of a child usually is. "Little Susan," as she was lovingly called, had married Ellis's Uncle James, who died and left her a widow with one child. Now Jimmie, five years old, named after his father, had been taken as well and Susan left empty-handed. Ellis's own heart ached in sympathy with her suffering. She made the clean, white garments for Jimmie herself and placed them upon his still, cold body.

With a heavy heart she went back to school. What else was there for her to do now, but try to improve her time the best she could? She had reached a dead-end point, a dismal flat plain with no shining peaks to break the horizon. She must pick up her faith and go on, though it seemed to Ellis there was no place to go: Her young life was leading nowhere.

3

Bard and Brigham

The summer of 1865 proved to be extremely hot and unpleasant. There had been no rain for many weeks. The farmers' faces were creased with worry, the women very tense and still. Could they live through another drought if it came to that? They carefully measured the contents of their larders, said their prayers, and bided their time.

In July Brigham Young himself paid the city of Mount Pleasant a visit. There were many settlements scattered through Utah now. Brigham tended to them all like a diligent father, and with his phenomenal mind remembered the names of Brother Johnson's boy who got married last summer, Sister Farnsworth's daughter he blessed the last time he was through, Sister Adams's delicious apple dumplings. He was their prophet on a very personal level, and everywhere he went his people loved him.

They prepared for his visit now with excited fervor, the women putting their houses in order, washing and mending their best clothing; the men clearing their yards, repairing fences, making sure the gate on its hinges hung true. The night Brigham's group arrived a party was given. Ellis attended escorted by Amasa Tucker.

There were many leading brethren there she knew. It was good to dance with Brother Richards and feel so at ease, so accepted and known. She was introduced to a Brother Henry Brizzie who drew her into conversation and learned of her burning desire to return to Battle Creek. For Ellis the evening proved successful. She went home with happy heart and flushed cheeks.

The following morning hundreds gathered at the new bowery, simple people who had laid their work aside, turned their backs on the persistent demands of their daily living, and come with open hearts to hear Brother Brigham's words. When he arose to address them a stillness seemed to hover, a wonderful stillness, warm and calm. He spoke a beautiful sermon to the people and praised the progress they'd made since his last visit there. Then he bade them be of good cheer, and he made them a promise. The men sat a little straighter, some leaned forward; women sought one another's eyes.

"Your crops shall not be lost," he promised. "You shall have rain to make this promise true, and it will come down abundantly before you leave this bowery."[1]

His bold words seemed to ring in the stillness that followed. Ellis sat with the others and heard the words. And with the others she watched the clouds gather, heard the gentle drum of the steady rain. The rejoicing among the people was almost reverent. "Their efforts would not be fruitless now," Ellis explained. "Their children would be fed, their hearts were comforted, their faith strengthened and their souls rejoiced."[2]

Throughout the day Ellis had noticed the President's gaze upon her. It puzzled her that he should watch her so. She had never seen him except at the pulpit or in an assembly. Between meetings Brother Brizzie caught her and surprised her with an offer of a seat in his carriage if she wished to ride with him back to Pleasant Grove. He had taken her by surprise; she demurred a little, saying she would speak to her father about the matter.

A celebration was held that same evening. Ellis was personally introduced to Brigham Young. He invited her to dance, but the floor filled quickly, so they stood at the side together and watched the dance. Several people, sensing the situation, offered the President and his partner their place, but Brigham declined. Instead he took Ellis to a seat and sat down beside her. He inquired about her life and about her family, especially Grandfather Hawley.

William Hawley had been cut off from the Church for some disagreement, some misbehavior — a thing not uncommon, especially at that time. In fact, the entire city of Pleasant Grove had become immersed in inner quarrels, accusing one another of petty offenses, confessing old pre-baptism sins, drumming up courts on the flimsiest charges. Brigham had finally instructed the whole town to be rebaptized, and this cleared the air considerably. But William Hawley's name had come up with a number of others while he was on one of his trips back east, when he couldn't defend himself or clear the charges. It incensed him that he was cut off this way, and the humiliation and injustice of it kept him out of the Church for years.

Ellis did her best to defend her grandfather to the prophet, trying to soften any prejudice he might have. He asked if her father was there, said he'd like to meet him. She was amazed at the ease she felt in his presence. Her natural timidity dissolved before his kindness, the fatherly feel of his manners and words.

It was time for the next dance to start; they walked out together. She whirled through the merry paces on his arm, aware that all eyes in the room were upon them. She was honored, her young pride was touched, her heart thrilled. But her good and sensitive nature was also stirred. That night in her prayers she thanked her Heavenly Father for his goodness to her, that she had become "the object and interest of so good and great a man."[3]

The following day Ellis discussed Brother Brizzie's proposal with her father, sincerely wishing his counsel. He told her wisely, "Ellis, if I thought he wanted you to go and no further, that his interest is only that of a friend, I would not object. And will not now if it is your wish to go, understanding what you do. But I think that he has other motives; in short, I believe he wants a wife."

Ellis, in part, had sensed the same thing. "I do want to go to Battle Creek," she responded, "but not under such circumstances. I'm glad this is your answer."[4]

She gave Brother Brizzie her answer and sat through the meeting, the last session before the visiting group would disperse and go their separate ways. At the close of the meeting while she and her father stood talking with "Little Susan," the President spied them, left the group he was talking to on the stand, came over and asked for an introduction. He was surprised to learn that this man was Ellis's father; he would sooner have thought him her brother — and said so.

"I understand you are going to the city," he said.

She assured him she was not. Then, calm as summer, he invited her to go to Salt Lake with him! Her heart froze, she stammered, trying to gather her thoughts now.

"I'm going to school," she told him, "and I would not like to leave that." She trembled at the magnitude of the idea — and at something else. Zebulon Jacobs lived there. She couldn't bear the thought that he might believe she was chasing after his attentions. Brigham stood and watched her clear features for a moment, clouded now by fear and self-doubt.

"If you will come with me," he said, his tones full and measured, "you shall go to school and be as one of my own children."[5]

This was more than Ellis could take in so quickly. "I will do as my father says," she murmured.

"You may do as you please to do, Ellis," her father replied.

How could she refuse now? What would Brigham think if she refused him? She was frightened to say yes — but terrified to say no. "I will go," she told him.[6]

One of his carriages stood near them. He instructed the driver to take Ellis to her home and return in half an hour. The thing was done! What madness, what wonder! She ran in to the family, who grew instantly excited at hearing her news. There was so little time for preparation — less for farewells!

They drove to Spring Town that evening and stopped at the bishop's. Brigham was solicitious of Ellis's welfare, spoke kindly to her, made a point of introducing her to other members of the company. How she maintained her composure she hardly knew. Why was she plagued with this awful natural shyness? The next morning Brigham told her she could return home and get anything she might have forgotten, since he would be holding a meeting there that morning. She did so, grateful for the chance to see her father once more. He gave her much kind parting counsel and advice.

There were more stops, more meetings, more people to meet and smile at. Fort Ephraim . . . Manti . . . Moroni. Ellis was riding in the President's own carriage. She noted that Brigham seemed in a deep study. Suddenly he turned to his wife who was sitting beside him.

"What girl was it Zeb was engaged to down south here somewhere?"

The question shot like a bolt through Ellis. Brigham was looking searchingly at her!

His wife replied, "I don't know, but when Chariton comes up you can ask him."

Ellis sat, hardly breathing, hardly moving. When Chariton rode up her heart nearly stopped beating. But it seemed they had forgotten the dreaded question. It was long minutes before she could breathe with relief again.[7]

On July 17 they arrived in Payson. The next day Brigham told Ellis she could stop at Battle Creek with Brother Musser, who would be staying all night there. They could join the party the following morning at Lehi. She jumped at the chance to go home, to see her grandparents. What a fuss they made when they learned her news! Grandma Ellis set instantly about repairing her wardrobe, adding to her scanty, unsatisfactory store.

The days were long and the traveling tedious but at last — too soon — they pulled into Salt Lake City. It was the middle of the day. The dusty carriages rolled through the sweeping arms of the Eagle Gate, making the entrance to Brigham's estate. She had seen the Beehive House before; she had actually been inside once as Zebulon's guest. But that was just briefly, in a whirl, a romantic daze. Could she really be coming to live in this elegant building? She stood in the shade of the long pillared porch. What lay waiting for her? How she dreaded being introduced to the family! How she feared they would reject and look down upon her.

As the President led me in the house, introducing me to members of his family as they came out to meet him, my heart beat almost audibly. Among his welcomers was a middle-aged lady with kind and noble countenance. He made us acquainted and said, "Lucy, this is her home and I want you to be a mother to her."[8]

Lucy, not missing a beat, ushered her young guest into a cool, pleasant sitting room, sat down and conversed for awhile to ease her reception. Then she excused herself to attend to some household duties. Ellis was alone in the small, still room, with the harpsichord and the mother-of-pearl table. Will I make friends, she wondered, or how will it be?

In the evening Sister Lucy informed her that the family always met at the Lion House for prayers. Would she like to go over? Ellis said she would be pleased to.

The Lion House stood right next door. In fact, the two houses had a connecting passage. Ellis walked down the endless hall with the six family members, her heart in her throat, her head held high.

The Lion House parlor was elegantly furnished, with brilliant chandeliers that cast sparkles and shadows. Ellis found a seat as quickly as she could, painfully aware of the eyes upon her and the speculations that floated around the room. What motive did Brigham have in bringing her here? After a while Ellis found the courage to glance around her.

The room was crowded to its utmost capacity, every sofa and chair having an occupant. The President was sitting near a table on the west side of the room. At his right hand sat Sister Eliza R. Snow and Zina. The latter, as our eyes met, smiled and bowed and then came over and shook hands, kindly welcoming me — a moment that was not unnoticed by the President.[9]

When prayers were over and they went back, Ellis retreated to the most obscure corner of the room she could find, hoping, should Brigham come in, that he would not see her. She had not been seated long before he did come, carrying in his hand a small light. He spoke a few words to Lucy, then looked around until his eyes caught sight of the slim, dark girl. He walked over and, with a smile, sat down beside her.

"I thought I was bringing you to a place where you'd never been."

"Oh no," she confessed, "I have been here once before."

"Well," he replied, "when we were riding along in Sanpete it struck me that you were the girl."

He was curious now; he asked several questions. She answered all of them promptly and readily.

"There is no engagement between you now and I am glad of it," Brigham concluded. "If he should wish to renew his attentions, have nothing to say to him, Ellis."

How relieved she was! She explained her fears, her hesitancy to accept his offer on this account. Kindly Brigham reassured her, told her to let nothing of the kind cause her unpleasant feelings. He wanted her to feel perfectly at home, and assured her she could start school as soon as she wished.[10]

After he left Sister Lucy offered to show Ellis to her room. They walked up the elegant staircase together, the staircase that twisted and wound through the air, gracefully unsupported by frame or column. The rich, soft carpet swallowed the sound of their steps. Could this be home to her? Her brain was too tired to answer the hundred questions that whirled inside. Gratefully she slept. She could wait till tomorrow. Today had been more than enough; she was glad it was through. She knew she could face her unknown future if that's how she took it — one tomorrow, just one new tomorrow at a time.

During the first few days Ellis had some difficulty adjusting. There were many hours of loneliness, even tears. On July 20 Oscar Young was married and a big celebration was held in the house. She stayed in her room most of the day, lonely and crying. That same evening, though, she accompanied the President to a Mormon Battalion party, which she enjoyed. The following day Zeb called to see her. They conversed on a casual basis awhile, then talked tentatively of their past, returned old letters, and agreed to part as friends.

On July 22 Brigham surprised her with the gift of a lovely white muslin dress. He meant for her to wear it at a grand ball being held on July 24, which he wished her to attend as his partner. There was a dressmaker in the home who assisted her with alterations and fittings. Ellis had never before looked so beautiful, so vivacious. She had matured into an elegant, graceful woman. Her delicate features were finely chiseled, and in the bloom of youth, with her dark hair and brilliant eyes, she cut a truly beguiling figure.

Ellis called the ball "a decided success."[11] She met many of her friends there, including Milford, with whom she shared an enjoyable dance.

Ellis's feelings about Brigham Young at this time are not hard to discover. They were not in any way clouded or confused. Although his attentions seem to us personal in nature — escorting her to gala public affairs, engaging her daily in intimate, long conversations, presenting her with small favors and gifts — she found nothing suspect or unnatural in his behavior. She spoke often of Brigham's ability, though engaged with much weightier matters, to be aware of a young girl's feelings and needs, her desire for beautiful things to wear. And it was not only Ellis to whom Brigham gave gifts. His own daughters received new dresses as well. After the evening spent with Brigham at the ball Ellis recorded:

> I indeed felt pleased, but I am assured I did not feel vain, for deep down in my soul was a humble and fervent desire ever to prove worthy of the association of the truest and best of God's noblemen, and that of His purest, more intelligent daughters.[12]

She called him her "beloved, her honored foster father,"[13] and paid him a tribute which, even after years, rings with the warmth of sincerity.

> How kind and fatherly Brigham Young was to me. My heart warms and my eyes moisten to the big heart, the generous consideration of that great man who lived to bless all the world as far as mortal power could reach. Directed by what seemed a divine instinct he could read and understand the human heart. His vision could encompass all of mortal need in the great and vital things, and even unto the smallest detail of everyday life.[14]

Ellis started school the following Monday. With her quick discernment it did not take her long to discover what a rare man she had for a teacher. Karl G. Maeser was a German convert, the first convert from Saxony, "reared and educated under superior masters in that land of traditional intellectual love."[15] He had arrived in the

Salt Lake Valley in 1860, opened a school in the Fifteenth Ward called the Deseret Lyceum — tuition $6.00 per quarter, in advance.

But there were very few people committed to education and the Maesers' existence was hand to mouth. In 1862 Brigham appointed Professor Maeser to take charge of the Union Academy, but conditions did not improve much for him. This noble man, intelligent, cultured, used to luxury and high regard, was reduced to the lowest extremities. His son, Reinhard, wrote:

> He knew what it was to be hungry; he knew what it was to shiver with his loved ones on Christmas Day. It is reported that on one occasion in Salt Lake City, at a party, during the intermission for supper, he announced to the people, "If any of you have anything you do not care for, Brother Maeser will be glad for something to eat."
>
> At times conditions became so distressing that the professor felt impelled to make a personal canvass of those who owed him, to collect on tuition whatever his debtors might be able to share with him; he would accept anything usable in the household. On these errands he took his wheelbarrow but, more frequently than not, he returned home as he had left — with his barrel empty. "Well," he would say, "the poor people are no better off than we. They can't pay; I forgive them."[16]

In 1864 Brigham, undoubtedly aware of Maeser's struggles, appointed him private tutor to his own children. Maeser was able for the first time to both eat and teach. And Ellis was able to partake of the wealth of intelligence and knowledge she had hungered for since she was a child.

Although she was less advanced than the other pupils, Ellis caught on to the studies and advanced rapidly. Maeser would often mark her grammar and composition recitations "best." This pleased her and made her more anxious yet to excel. School was a source of joy; she loved the sensation of learning something new every day. She could feel her inner powers expanding as her personal horizons expanded and grew.

Just a few weeks after her arrival in the city, a holiday in the school term came round. Brigham, with his intuitive understanding, asked if she would like a little visit to Pleasant Grove. She replied "joyfully and spontaneously."[17] The following morning he sent his carriage to collect her, driven by his son, Chariton Jacobs. Chariton was not only skillful in handling the spirited horses, but an "eloquent conversationalist."[18]

The trip was a delight to Ellis, perhaps more so because she knew what awaited her: the "grand old New England hospitality" of her grandparents' home. The visit, she said, was like "a step into heaven."[19]

> Here I had come, homesick and mother sick, longing for the touch of a kindred spirit, and their encouraging words, tender kisses, and embraces and sweetest sympathy were healing balm to my youthful soul.[20]

Friends and relatives, hearing of her arrival, dropped in to visit, warming her with their love much more than they knew, renewing her store of self-confidence and courage. When she returned to Salt Lake the Beehive House seemed suddenly dear, and everything bright and exciting again. She attended a production of "Camille" in the Salt Lake Theatre which featured Julia Dean Hayne as leading lady. The magic world was still there and she was part of it; she felt for the first time as though she might really belong.

This opportunity for a new life was timely. Ellis had lived through some morbid and trying years. She could feel now the balance wheel turning, changing, dissolving her "sorrowfully vague mentality,"[21] helping her to a safe equilibrium where her own inner beauties and strengths could at last have play.

In a very intimate way she was part of the household, exchanging whispered secrets with the girls, sympathizing with boyish complaints, writing poems — verses of love to be sent out on scented notes. Her poetry must have progressed to a competent level because the other girls came flocking for Ellis to write their verses.

She mentions the names of some of her favorites of Brigham's children: John W., Willard, Maria and Phoebe, Susa, and "sweet, angelic Fannie."[22] She was also close to Emmeline Wells and her daughters, and to the children of Parley P. Pratt. Eliza R. Snow and Zina Huntington Young, Heber C. Kimball and George Q. Cannon, Wilford Woodruff and Franklin D. Richards — all were her friends. She had the association of God's noblemen and noble women and was learning how to hold her own, learning that they would love and accept her and have faith in her promising qualities.

Near the first of September her father and her younger brother, James, arrived in Salt Lake on business and came to visit her. She was overjoyed to see them, but she had changed. Their presence did not throw her into an agony of emotion. She was beginning to learn who she was and to find her own place. She could let go now, just a little, without so much suffering.

School continued to be a pleasure and a challenge, and more than that, an awakening.

> As a pupil of Professor Maeser how blessed was my life! Every moment in his presence seemed a benediction, so great was his spiritual influence, his intuitive uplift to all that was pure and divine. He was by nature spiritualistic. His implicit faith in *The Living God* was an integral part of his being, indeed the dominant spark of his magnetic influence over mind and morals.[23]

Here Ellis was again, seeing into the deepest that others had to offer, sensing their motives, reading their hearts. This man who was to establish Brigham Young Academy and be widely known for the brilliance and morality of his educational philosophies, had already been discovered by Ellis Reynolds, and afforded his due credit and reverence and love.

> Under his superior tutelage I realized a truly great blessing in sharing the immensity of his knowledge, his power to impart the wealth of his intelligence and superior wisdom to the world about him. He helped me to higher ideals in so many ways. I knew he was often tried and his heroic efforts at self-control were an object lesson never to be forgotten. His personal suggestions and wise direction of effort have proven beacon lights shining ever brighter as years go on.[24]

Ellis experienced not only a spiritual and intellectual awakening, but a cultural, artistic awakening as well. Her main experience with the arts had been country productions of amateur plays in the local schoolhouse. Now she would dress for the evening and, in company with Fannie and Phoebe, drive to the lovely new theatre, pass through the entrance — thirty-two feet wide and twenty feet high, supported by two elegant Grecian Doric columns — sit in the family's reserved box seats, and give herself entirely to the glittering world of wonder before her.

The theatre, itself, was beautifully appointed with elaborate ceiling work, lace filigree gracing the boxes, an unusually deep stage apron, and a wide drop curtain encased in an elegant frame. The drop curtains were works of art in themselves. Ellis could sit and gaze at the "Return of The Victorious Fleet" and imagine herself standing beside one of the tall Roman columns watching the long boats move through the still, bright water.

The home company consisted of several brilliant artists: David McKenzie, Phil Marget, Dunbar Sarah Alexander, and Margaret Clawson among them. They opened a Pandora's box of sensations for Ellis, who had difficulty divorcing the scenes before her—the wild beauty, the throbbing emotion—from reality. What she saw and felt were too potent to be make-believe.

"Indeed, what a wonderful unfolding of intelligences to a half-starved intellect,"[25] she recorded as Shakespeare's array of characters came into her vision. But of all the grand heroes and heroines he had created, the man himself claimed her deepest devotion and awe.

> William Shakespeare—he to me seemed the most remarkable of all his heroes in all of his varied life scenes, so vividly depicted by the genius of real men and women.[26]

Ellis, though treading new ground, at first with caution, could not for long keep her own brilliant spirit down. With characteristic perception it drew her deeper.

> I began to make a study of the relative powers of the representatives of the histrionic art and flattered myself I could detect even little flaws in their acting and very fully appreciate their praiseworthy powers of delineation. I seemed to understand that an intuitive insight into human nature must be inborn to enable an individual to impersonate the finer emotions of the soul so perfectly in facial expression, in gesture, in the vibration and modulation of the voice. . . .[27]

So the theatre became a true art form to Ellis Reynolds, who had a way of grasping the fine things in life and incorporating them thoroughly into her being, so that their light and beauty refined and reflected her own.

Although her schedule now was varied and busy, Ellis didn't lose touch with old friends, Flora Shipp among them. While spending an afternoon with Flora at the Shipp home, Ellis confided that she had seen Flora's brother "but once since I have been here."[28] It seemed that Milford would ever be a topic of concern in their discussions.

A few weeks later Ellis attended a theatre production with Maggie Curtis and Maria Young. Excitedly they gazed over the parquet to see what they could discover in the "sea of faces" around them. Ellis recognized Milford's face, so familiar, so handsome. But he sat with Flora and his mother, and his young wife sat on the opposite side of the theatre with her father. What could this portend? Her companions whispered tales of how unkind he had been to his wife. Ellis, eyes sparking fire, defended his honor. She wouldn't believe it — she couldn't believe such things of him.

On November 19 Ellis called on Miss Shipp again. Milford was there, and he appeared very low in spirit. Ellis watched him, wondering. Suddenly he remarked, "It's not all life to live, nor all death to die."

From some spark of defiance within her she answered him quickly, repeating a line he often had quoted to her, "Is it all happiness to get married?"

He met her dark eyes. "That is a hard question to answer," he replied slowly.[29] Instantly Ellis regretted her flippant unkindness. His eyes could appear so mournful, so lost and deep. That night Flora told her his wife had left him.

Ellis returned to her own peaceful room in the Beehive House, not yet ready to unravel her inner responses, nor face what that separation might mean to her.

Life in Brigham Young's home was a haven for her. "Here there were no discords," she said. "This home circle was the pattern of comfort, order, and refinement — the abode of love, sweet peace, and divine progression, the blessed offspring of a supreme faith, noble industry, and beautiful unselfishness. There was no lavish expenditure and yet no need was unprovided for."[30] Such praise from Ellis was praise indeed. Her sensitive, questing spirit always saw deeply and reflected what she saw with alarmingly honest clarity.

Besides the peace and integrity this home provided came something else Ellis needed: a noble example. Lucy Decker had been Brigham's first polygamous wife. She was the mistress of the elegant Beehive House; poised, gracious, and dignified — and much more.

> Sister Lucy Decker Young, the queen of this home, was a most exemplary, wise, lovable woman, so just and sweet and kind to "the stranger within her gates." Never can I forget her motherly watchful care of me and the beautiful, useful lessons I learned in government of children, in management of the modernized home — industry, frugality, bringing such wonderful results from a small beginning, phenomenal self-control, and freedom from petty gossip. So like my own dear mother — seeing the good in everything.[31]

Brigham and his family applied well on a practical level the principles he taught his people. Much of this practical application took root in Ellis and became part of her lifelong philosophy. The government of children, home management, "phenomenal self-control" she saw here and did her best to copy — these came to her aid time and time again in moments of need.

With the approach of the holidays Ellis felt herself longing to be "home" in Battle Creek with the people she loved. Brigham consented to her desires and Christmas Eve found her safe in her grandparents' warm, cozy quarters again. Then began what she called "a series of the happiest, most exciting, brilliant days I ever experienced."[32]

Christmas morning she went sleigh riding with Parley Driggs, sailing over the crisp, sparkling snow, feeling young and at peace with the world. She ate a hearty noon meal with her grandparents at Uncle Asa's. Soon after they returned, Otto Mayhew and Milford Shipp called to see her. It seemed Milford had yielded to the same allurement as she, to spend the holidays at dear old Pleasant Grove. Or had he learned from his sister that Ellis would be there?

That evening a party was held and they met again. She was surrounded by many dear old friends. But that was not what brought the color to her cheeks. Milford was being remarkably attentive. There seemed a depth of meaning in every word, every glance he gave her. Near the end of the evening he contrived a few moments alone and begged for a private interview. Should she grant it? She couldn't see that much harm could be done, so she consented.

He arranged to call for her at ten the following morning. Although she was fatigued with excitement she did not sleep. She knew that at last the moment had arrived — the moment she had longed for and feared, and dreamed and imagined — for years, ever since she had been a young, awkward girl. She went over in her mind every word of their last conversations. In memory she thought over the long, stormy years. It had been such a short time since his wife left him. Why did he, how could he express such affection for her?

At last she concluded that if, as she thought, he approached her, her answer would be in the negative. She knew that the President was unfavorably prejudiced against him. So was her grandmother, who had opposed even this brief meeting. She could pacify her grandmother by saying that Milford wished to know the nature of Brigham Young's feelings toward him. It would never be so easy to pacify Brigham himself.

At ten o'clock she drove with Milford to her Aunt Laura's. Aunt Laura gave them a private room. They conversed for a moment or two upon commonplace topics. Milford must have had some misgivings about how to begin, how to explain himself to the wide-eyed girl before him. At last he began to unfold his feelings to her, "all the particulars of his wife's desertion, how he had loved her, and of his vain and useless pleadings."[33] Milford, using his brilliant way with words, brought into play all his power and poignancy. Ellis's tender heart was softened; it was hard to keep the tears from her eyes.

"I loved my wife," he told her, his rich voice gentle, "but my religion and my God I love better than all on earth."[34]

He had touched that response he had always had power to draw from her, rekindled the adoration, the spiritual love. The old feelings of resentment left her, the objections she had so carefully formed were gone. "Truly," she recorded, "a man so noble was worthy of woman's deepest and purest love."[35]

He was free now to go on; he pushed his advantage. From their very first acquaintance, she must know, he had felt deeply for

her, although he had tried to ignore it. So many times he had
thought to declare his love, but something would happen to thwart
his designs, to waylay his plans and directions. He brought up the
delicate subject of Sanpete. He had resolved, he said, to bare his
heart to her at that meeting, but fate and her own ignorance had
intervened and he was denied again.

She remembered too well the awkward mix-up of partners,
her own guilty pain. He longed for sympathy, he told her, someone to cheer and comfort his heart. He spoke with his beautiful
eyes upon her, drawing her, holding her prisoner in their gaze.
"Oh Ellis," he said, "will you not be to me that sunshine that will
dispel all clouds from my heart?"[36]

He took her hand; he knew from her eyes she could not deny
him. All was revealed between them now. Nothing that was past
could stand in their way. Only one negative thought marred the
moment for Ellis: What would Brigham Young say? She knew how
strong Brigham's feelings were, how adverse he was to changing
settled opinions. How could she contrive his consent to their
union?

It was the one blemish, the one dark cloud on her horizon of
light.

It was the day after Christmas, but for Ellis the celebration
was just beginning. That evening she accompanied Milford to a
private party held at Aunt Lucy's. She was already beginning to
think of him as her Bard, his second name and one used affectionately by those closest to him. Many of her friends who were at the
party responded unkindly, even bitterly, toward him and toward
what Ellis regarded as her own "good news." This was painful for
her to see. Her own allegiance had been entirely turned, whole-
heartedly won.

> I loved him so devotedly — the love that had slumbered for
> years was now awakened to a new and holy life. I know that the
> object of my devotion was good and noble, that his principles were
> pure, his integrity unsullied. How uncharitable is all mortality![37]

Perhaps the event was a little intimidating, for the following
day she and Milford agreed not to say much to one another in

public. He even thought she should accept invitations from other men. Consequently Ellis went sleigh riding that evening with Frank B. What her feelings were can only be guessed at.

Another day of quiet separation followed. She spent most of the time with her old friend, Lydia Robinson, who had recently married. The evening she spent at home with Grandma Hawley.

The following evening, however, a grand military ball had been planned. Ellis attended and probably missed Milford's presence less than she had anticipated. The gentlemen were decked out in uniforms and the ladies resplendent in white dresses with ribbons of red, white, and blue. Ellis received her share of attention and admiration, admiration that came from sincere and loving hearts. It warmed her own heart, or perhaps it was frosting to the cake of the secret happiness no one else knew.

December 30 was a Saturday. Ellis spent the day at her cousin Susan's. Milford was there, but they could not openly converse. So they contrived another, more amorous method. He would write something in the little book he carried in his pocket and then pass it to Ellis occasionally. She would write something back and return it to him.

It is charming to think of Ellis so occupied. She was not quite nineteen years old; she was young and romantic. Milford, on the other hand, was a man of twenty-nine. But remembering his own romantic nature, his dreamy, idealistic approach to life, perhaps this occurrence was not really out of keeping.

That evening a party was held at the Robinson farm. Milford was there, and Ellis felt whole and happy. In her own beautiful, glowing terms she described the night:

> I shall never forget the brilliant loveliness of that night. The air was sharp and cold and chilly. The moon shone in her brightest glory. Stars emitted their choicest beams, and scintillant drops of frost, glittering in the moonbeams, descended from heaven to their vast bed of snow beneath. The sublime magnificence of the scene filled the soul with a solemn awe and admiration.[38]

On the last day of the year she ate dinner at Uncle Benjamin's, then spent the remainder of the evening with the other young folk at Aunt Mary's. They were all writing on slates, so she and Milford

were able to exchange some words. He expressed his desire for
them to be quickly united. Ellis asked what he thought of the pro-
bability of his wife's returning to him. He responded that he
thought it unlikely. This seemed to encourage her. With that as-
surance perhaps Brigham's support could be more readily won.

January 1, 1866: a new year before her. She was nearly nineteen, and at last her future had come. At last she knew who she
was and where she was headed. Love — that spiritual union, for
which she expressed such a need throughout her life — had at last
arrived to fill the dark corners of doubt and emptiness within her.

This first day of the year was spent at Aunt Lydia's, and there
was a ball again in the evening. The next day Milford returned to
Provo. Ellis and Parley Driggs's cousin accompanied him.

As they attempted to cross the frozen Provo River the ice
cracked and one of the sleigh runners broke through. The sleigh
rapidly began sinking. There were some frightened moments as
they scrambled out together, found a log and crossed to the other
side. Bard gave her his hand and pulled her onto the firm shore
safely, then held her gaze with his own shining eyes and said,
"May I lead you through life's journey?"[39]

It was a romantic question, but it was sincerely meant. And
the journey they had already begun would be a long one, filled
with more pain and hardship than either knew.

After a few hours Ellis and her companion left him. Milford
carefully tucked the wrappings around her and said good-bye. Even
a parting of a few days' time seemed painful to her. She looked
behind, watching until he was lost to view.

On January 5 Ellis attended another military ball, this one in
American Fork. She felt distant and lonely, removed from the
gaiety bubbling around her. The evening passed somewhat slowly
for her until, near ten o'clock, a girl from the far end of the hall
came over, bent down and whispered something in her ear.

Ellis's cheeks immediately colored. Her eyes, which had
looked preoccupied, started to shine. Bard had come! In a few
moments he was beside her, handsome and tall, with that thick
dark hair she loved to touch and those eyes that entranced her. Her
joy was all the greater because it was unexpected. But she was
always to feel that way when he entered a room; he was always to

have that power to thrill her emotions, to make her long for his approval and his love.

On January 9 Ellis returned to the city. Her courtship had been brief but idyllic. Now reality came flooding back upon her. She "trembled as to the uncertainty of her fate."[40] What would the President say?

It seems obvious that she was not eager to find out. She met Milford occasionally at his sister's. But one evening he came to her at the Beehive House. They talked together in the small front sitting room, the same room where Ellis had sat stiffly her first day there, frightened and uncertain, unable to see around the corners to what her tomorrows would be. Now Milford sat here beside her, with the beauty she found so incredible, with the love that was like a new-formed miracle in her heart.

While they sat thus, Amelia Young chanced in upon them, closing the door very quickly once she saw them. But Ellis steeled herself for what would be coming. Certainly Amelia would tell Brigham what she had seen. Certainly Brigham would call her to an accounting.

The very next morning Brigham approached her when she was alone. There were no preliminaries; he wasted no time. He began, "Mr. Shipp was here to see you last night, was he?"

"Yes, sir." Her voice was soft, but its tone rang true.

"Well, I want to tell you before it is too late that I would have nothing to do with him."[41]

He then expounded, pointing out all of Milford's abuses. Milford's trespasses seemed to center around his wife and his treatment of her. As she listened Ellis knew how thoroughly Brigham's mind had been prejudiced against him. She was in an agony. She had no desire to offend this man who had been so kind to her, who had given so much of himself to make her happy. Yet she carried that inner confidence; she knew "that if he knew Milford Shipp's inmost heart he would have no objections — he would love him as a son."[42]

But Brigham did not know. All Ellis could do was pray that the clouds might be lifted, and meanwhile hold firm so that Brigham knew how resolved she was to marry Milford.

She was patient. The long weeks passed. On April 5 her

father arrived in the city. "My kind and dear affectionate father! In my heart there is a love that exists for him too deep for expression."[43]

Five days later Milford approached William Reynolds and formally asked his consent to marry his daughter. This was not exactly what her father wanted for Ellis, but he consented. He could see how deeply she wanted this.

Meanwhile, the quiet miracle was occurring. Very few people could change Brigham's mind once he had set it. Ellis used sweet persuasion and prayer. When he saw where her heart was, his opposition softened. She appealed to him, her dark intelligent eyes clear and guileless. "I do not wish to do anything," she told him, "without your blessing."

He knew how sincerely she meant it. The feeling between them, which had sprung into life so spontaneously, had matured into true regard for each other. Brigham knew what a rare young woman she was. Perhaps with prophetic brilliance he guessed at her future. Perhaps he feared for her security.

Whatever his feelings were he put them aside now and gave her the one gift she craved at his hands. "You shall ever have my blessing, Ellis," he promised.[44]

The fifth day of May marked Milford's father's and mother's birthdays and wedding anniversary combined. Milford wanted his own marriage to Ellis to take place on this day. There were only three weeks left for preparation. Yet Ellis's means, or rather lack of means, kept extravagance down. During these last days she saw Milford often, savoring his words of love, his eager plans.

"How sweet to know," she breathed, "that you are beloved, and to feel that it is in your power to promote in any way the felicity and comfort of that being you hold most dear in life. Oh, methinks this earth affords no greater bliss."[45]

Milford realized what a prize he had in Ellis. To be forsaken by two wives would be a blow to any man's pride. When he met Ellis at Battle Creek he had been sad and despondent, disturbed that the good name he prized had come into disfavor. He had always been held in high esteem by the brethren. Now many minds had been biased against him, the foremost being that of the prophet himself.

When Milford saw that Ellis, in her pure enthusiasm, would love and trust him despite all the stories she'd heard, despite all the ups and downs of their past together, he was filled with gratitude as well as love. He said she "was as the sunlight bursting through the darkness of his sorrow."[46] He began to call her his "sunshine", just as her parents had called her their sunshine long years ago. Sunshine—a source of light and power; sustenance of a heavenly kind. Ellis's unique spirit was fashioned to give this kind of glowing strength to the people she loved.

> When he talked to me of his devotion, his perfect trust and confidence, my heart bounded with the purest, sweetest joy it had ever known. These professions are sacredly enshrined in the depths of my soul.[47]

So Ellis stated in the pleasure of her love. Everything had a spiritual dimension for Ellis; it was to enhance all she did, all she learned through life.

As the day for the wedding approached she felt calm and peaceful. Others might look on and judge her decision to be hasty —even foolish or unwise. But Ellis knew better. She might be young, but she was not untried. She might be romantic, but she was not shallow.

> From the time my promise was first given, my mind had dwelt seriously upon the step I was taking. I considered it in all its phases. I realized how uncertain is human happiness, and that a wife's position was serious and responsible. But I was confident I could be happy, for was not my future felicity depending on *Milford*—that truly noble man who to me was so endeared.[48]

Somehow, through all the disgrace and discrepancies of his recent career, she had maintained her idealistic vision of him.

> He was to me all that the enlivened fancy of girlhood or the mature judgment of women could picture in their imagination. So kind and affectionate, so faithful to the cause of Mormonism. So wise and intellectual and possessed of that fine intuitiveness so rarely found in the nature of man. He was ambitious, ardent, and energetic, all that was noble and laudable. In truth, I never saw a person who could so enchant and fascinate by the power of language.[49]

May 5, 1866, dawned clear and cloudless. Although Ellis had pictured in her mind that all brides would be nervous, even feeling a degree of sad inner thought, her own mind this morning was light and happy. Milford was to arrive around ten o'clock. Carefully she dressed herself in her wedding clothing—not satin robes, but plain white muslin. Then she slipped into the "longhall" at the head of the staircase, the lovely formal sitting room where she and Milford had spent many happy hours together.

The room possessed that graceful taste that was Brigham's genius: two elegant glass chandeliers hung from the ceiling, catching the early sun's rays and reflecting them back in scattered patterns along the carpet. A large piano sat against the west wall, one which had survived the journey across the plains. The gray-blue walls and the deep burgundy Victorian furniture set a restful, congruent tone to the place. Ellis drew in the peace like a cloak around her.

She knelt, desiring to offer one last petition that she might be blessed with a happy future, that she might glean knowledge and wisdom from life. She was reverent; it was a spiritual moment. She so much desired to be a true and faithful wife, one who would sustain her companion "by thought, word, and action and by constant and never-ending prayers."[50]

This prayer was a real experience for Ellis, one she would not forget for the rest of her life. "I think I never was so truly earnest in my communings with my Heavenly Father. Truly the spirit of light was showered upon me. My faith was implicit and there was a voice within whispering, 'Thy prayers shall be answered.' "[51]

As she rose to her feet her heart overflowed with joy. She opened the shutters on one of the windows that faced the street. She saw Bard walking up the hill, coming, storybook fashion, to claim her. She gazed upon him a moment, then flew back to her room and waited until she heard the doorbell ringing. As calmly as she could she descended the stair. He rose when he saw her enter, he gazed upon her, then with a beautiful smile extended his hand.

They walked to the Endowment House together. Heber C. Kimball performed the sacred rites. Ellis felt that the moment went deeper than ceremony, that their hearts were united in an "indissolvable tie, that all the vicissitudes of time or sorrow could not sever or unlink."[52] She truly believed that in life there are few such unions, but she knew that theirs was one, and she would strive for the remainder of her life to keep it so.

Following the marriage, the party retired to Mother Shipp's. Brigham and Lucy attended the celebration, as well as Brother Cannon and his wife. It was a "grand affair" as Ellis called it, with an array of tempting foods. The marble and silver cakes were most complimented, she mentioned.[53]

By seven o'clock the party had disbanded, and she and Milford started for home. *Home* . . . to Ellis the word was sacred. The idea of a home of her own, a home with this man, produced the deepest feelings within her. Cal and Flora had arranged the rooms for their reception. All was neat and cozy and homelike within. All her own trunks and private belongings had been transferred from Brigham's Beehive House to this new little home — not as beautiful or as comfortable, but surely as loved.

They entered the gates with a feeling of reverence and that first evening they knelt together in prayer, "in the first devotion of united hearts and aims"[54] that had found a safe abode with one another.

4

Marriage,
The Demanding Dream

The early days of her marriage were happy for Ellis. Since the ceremony took place on Saturday, the couple's first activity together was to attend church in the Eleventh Ward, whose boundaries extended south from South Temple to Third South Street and east from Sixth East to the edge of the city. The year after their marriage Camp Douglas became a fort and the ward was extended to include the military reservation.

Their own little adobe house was located at 34 South Seventh East. The chapel stood at the corner of Eighth East and First South streets. The bishop, Alexander McRae, whom Ellis called "a very notable and noble man and a natural guide and leader for his flock,"[1] had been a personal friend of the Prophet Joseph; at one time he had even shared imprisonment with him. He was to be bishop during the entire time Ellis lived there, through all the ups and downs of her varied life.

For a brief spell Ellis and Milford enjoyed the sweet solitude of each other's company to a degree not often experienced by newlyweds. Milford was working in his father's store. Their spare time they spent in reading, talking, taking walks together, sharing their joys, and counting their blessings.

But the stern realities of life can never be held long at bay. After many years of practicing Brigham's counsel of "feed the Indians, don't fight them," Indian troubles in southern Utah had climaxed. A number of men and boys working in the canyons had been murdered; in a few cases entire families had been killed. "Patience," Ellis recorded, "had ceased to be a virtue and the militia was called to the rescue."[2]

One afternoon Milford came rushing home from the store. He had been called to join the forces; he must leave in the morning. This was early summer and Ellis was just beginning her first pregnancy. Her feelings were somewhat on the surface. The separation was difficult for her. She recorded, "All hands must be busy in the needed preparation. All hearts much ache and in silence. No discouraging words must be uttered. Just work in faith."[3]

It was the first practical test of her high aspirations. She was helped through it by her mother-in-law. Mother Shipp knew of Ellis's desire to make a carpet, an old-fashioned rag rug like her mother had made. She sent over a wagonload of discarded clothing. Ellis was kept busy cutting off hooks and buttons, dainty trimmings, ribbons, and lace, which she worked into cushions and little nicknacks. The white pieces of material she took to a dyer; they were returned to her in bright, pretty colors. Sometimes she worked on the carpet late into the night, eager to have it completed for Milford's return. She was learning the blessing of work to a lonely heart.

In early autumn Ellis spent several weeks in Pleasant Grove, visiting her grandparents and seeing to her orchard, one of the wedding gifts her father had given her. She picked the fruit, then dried and canned it, pleased at the thought of seeing it safe upon her own shelves. While she was here the militia, marching triumphantly homeward, formed their third camp — in Pleasant Grove. Not one militiaman had been lost, and there was much rejoicing. Ellis found Milford and, once she was safe in his arms, it was difficult for her to let him go back to his company and proceed at their slow rate of march. She went on ahead with her boxes and sacks of fruit to prepare a welcome.

At last, after long, long days he was truly home, delighted by the surprise she had waiting. Nothing then — or ever through her life, would mean more to Ellis than Milford's praise and approval. It thrilled her heart when he would tell their friends in pride, "Ellis made this carpet!"[4]

During the bright autumn they did much visiting and entertaining. Although Milford was very occupied with his business and with Church duties in the evening, Ellis never complained. "I very early determined I would never deter him from any Church duty, however much I longed for his presence."[5] So she sat by her own clean hearth and blazing fire, happy and cozy — and occupied.

With materials Mother Shipp had kindly purchased — soft flannels, cambrics, linens, and gossamer batistes — she fashioned the little clothes she had so long dreamed of making. Sewing for her baby was to Ellis a near-sacred task. She was not prone to share it with others in any way.

> I could not let the casual eye look upon the little tiny things I fashioned day by day alone in all my glory of expectant motherhood! During this time I sat beside a table covered with a large cloth reaching to the floor, with my knitting work at hand, my other blessed work in a small basket when not in my hands. If a knock came at the door, under the table went my basket and the unfinished sock was in my hands and knitting needles clicking as I called out, "Come in."[6]

Winter was a season for rest and merrymaking. The crops had been garnered and supplies put in for the long, unproductive months ahead. The people could relax somewhat from the grueling discipline of pioneer living. Ellis did not mind missing the youthful festivities she was used to. The sweet influences, the joy, the "heavenly expectations"[7] far surpassed her earlier pleasures.

On February 24, 1867, a beautiful son was born to her. She was profuse in her spiritual gratitude and joy.

> My being seemed transported to the realms of purest, most perfect endeavor; an idealistic, heaven-inspired motherhood, in which to live for another without one selfish instinct save to bless this supreme gift from heaven which seemed so truly mine; to nourish, to cherish, to rear and mould and guide unto all the highest, holiest, exalted possibilities of earthly achievement. What sacred

mission for mortal woman to fill! I seemed to realize the supreme immensity, the unfathomed magnitude of the obligations and responsibilities accompanying this sacred, priceless gift of God, the Eternal Father.[8]

Through her life this reverence for motherhood persisted and was one of the driving forces behind all she was to achieve.

There followed long, restful days of convalescence while winter gave way to spring and the earth, renewed, rejoiced with her in hope and beauty. "In my unsophisticated soul it seemed the beginning of a real, continued happiness that could go on and on continually. The optimism of the youthful spirit had not really come to comprehend that mortal life had its ofttimes lessons of suffering and sorrow. I had listened, I had not learned the full meaning . . . of living in a world of probation. . . ."[9]

Her first trials as a mother were soon to come. Her little son, Milford Bard, named for his father, grew ill with whooping cough "in its worst type." She had seen too many children and infants die. There was no rest for her day or night as she watched his progress. And during these days of crisis, Milford was planning a move. He and his father had decided to open a branch store in Fillmore, Millard County. It would be a week's journey by wagon to reach their intended home. And in spite of little Bard's illness the plans went forward.

Somehow Ellis found herself perched on a wagon seat, with all her belongings piled in behind her, ready to try her fortunes in some strange place. There were actually two wagons, one driven by Milford and one by her brother, Asa. She sat, with her sick child in her arms, wondering what she was doing. "This unusual, unexpected migration in discomfort and anxiety far exceeded the pioneer journey of my early years. Then a carefree, optimistic child! Now a woman with all a woman's joys and hopes and responsibilities."[10]

But in this moment of trial Ellis's faith did not fail her. She remembered the promise that God would both hear and answer prayer. She prayed often as the wagon rolled along. Instead of the difficult trip being harmful for the baby, the fresh air seemed to work as a remedy. After the first two days he seemed to grow better, gradually gaining strength and health as they moved along. "My being o'er-flooded with humble gratitude," Ellis recorded.[11]

After nearly a week's travel they reached their destination, tired and weary, only to find that Milford's pre-made arrangements had fallen through. There were no accomodations ready for them, so they were forced to suffer the embarrassment of finding temporary help and lodging. The entire experience was distasteful to Ellis. Even once she was settled, she didn't feel happy and at home. Yet she was in love with Milford and more than ever determined to serve him, to support him in all he might wish to do. "My marriage vow must be held inviolate. I must be faithful and true whate'er should befall. Next to my allegiance to Heavenly Father it was so unto my companion."[12]

What might seem to the reader a naive, even extravagant view of the woman's role, was to Ellis a matter of deep personal conviction. This depth and power made it possible for her to endure what was yet to come.

During this winter in Fillmore Ellis's little sister, Anna Eliza, lived with her, thanks to her father who was willing to sacrifice Anna's help so that Ellis would have the companionship she needed. Together they fussed over and cared for the baby, took care of the household duties, knitted, and sewed, never neglecting even the smallest Church responsibility. Milford was required to make many trips back and forth to Salt Lake as he struggled to put the new store on a solid footing. There were very few friends or social activities in Fillmore. Ellis and Anna wrote many letters and read good books, trying to utilize their time constructively. They developed a deep, tender love for each other during these last brief, totally happy days.

March 3, Milford's thirty-second birthday, was approaching. Ellis was expecting his return from a trip to Salt Lake. She and Anna had put the house in perfect order. Ellis sat up late, awaiting his return, weaving her love into a beaded watch case she had been making. She finished it as she waited, tucked a little love verse carefully inside, then hung it in a spot where she hoped he would see it. A trifle, perhaps, but sprung from a loving heart.

As she sat in the cold, still night and waited, she thought of how deeply she loved this man, how she wanted to be a shining companion for him, worthy of his mental and spiritual powers. At last she heard his step on the walk. He was safe, he was home! She opened the door and greeted him, then moved into his arms. He held her close against him, her dark head on his shoulder. Then he whispered into her ear, "Ellis, my darling. I have accepted the mandates of the celestial law of marriage and will soon bring to our home a sister and companion for you."[13]

Her heart nearly stopped at the words. But how else could he say it? She was surprised, but she was calm; there was no weeping, no rejection, no condemnation from her. She had believed that this test of her faith would in time be hers. But here—so soon! So suddenly!

Two things gave Ellis strength to bear the ordeal. One was the depth of her feeling for Milford. She remembered their wedding day when their two hearts united in an "indissolvable tie that nothing could sever"[14]—*nothing*, no matter how harsh or severe.

"I wonder if it was a passion too much akin to worship," she wrote, "for to me he seemed almost divine. I could never believe he had one mortal weakness. He seemed so much a perfect, noble, honorable soul, in his judgment unerring, in his integrity and faithfulness to duty unfailing."[15]

The other force was her deep, real faith in her religion.

> But the bulwark of my strength was the faith in One all wise and powerful, the Eternal Creator of heaven and earth and all therein. I resolved in all humility, in my hope and trust and unwavering faith, to live this principle righteously, even to sharing the love, the attention, the very life of my heart's beloved, with another woman.
>
> The world has long since proclaimed this cruelty sacrilege, but with all my soul I believed it to be a most true and righteous principle, else I could not have under any condition accepted and become reconciled to its practice. Oh never, no never! could I have thus received it and tried so faithfully, hopefully, even cheerfully, to live its principles—to receive other women into my sacred shrine of Home.[16]

Even so, the night Milford married Margaret Curtis, Ellis—pregnant, nearing the birth of her second child—stood at her window all night long. Her deep feeling for him was now more enemy than friend. It made every aspect of her suffering so much more intense! It prevented her from realizing the spiritual ideal she forced herself to strive for.

On April 11 Ellis's second son was born. She named him William Austin, in honor of her dear grandfather Hawley, her own father, and her younger brother. Grandmother Ellis came the long miles to be near her, nursing her body skillfully, and with her remarkable power lifting Ellis's spirit. She had personal knowledge of the trial her young granddaughter faced. Her own husband had taken a second wife. How Ellis Hawley bore the trial is best expressed in the tribute paid her by Sarah Ellis, daughter of his second wife, named both for her own mother Sarah, and for this woman:

> When it came to the real test that tried women's souls in those days of the Church, the test of polygamy, she had been a queen. My mother was young and lovely when my father married her, but that older woman did not treat her as a supplanter—as she certainly had no thought of being—but more like a daughter and loved her children as her own, and the years cemented them together in trials and mutually-borne afflictions till they were not to be separated only by death. Our house was known as a house of peace, and it took three wise people to make it so![17]

The business venture in Fillmore did not prosper as Bard had expected. At last he admitted defeat and returned home. Ellis was overjoyed to be back in Salt Lake. Milford remodeled the old home to make it somewhat larger and more comfortable, though it was never to be large enough to meet their needs. Ellis immersed herself in her experiences as a mother, overwhelmed by some of the emotions her children awakened within her.

> I felt I would sacrifice everything just to know how to give them the best care, that they might live to manhood and in the strength and fruition of mind and body be ever near, with a continued cheering uplift and inspiration that I had sensed so very strongly ever since their birth.[18]

This desire, through the years, would mature and strengthen until it caught spark and became part of the burning flame that was to inspire her life's work.

While Milford was far away on a business trip to New York tragedy struck them. Little Willie became sick and nothing seemed to help him. Day by day he grew weaker before Ellis's watching eyes. He "began to pine," as she put it, "like a lovely lily flower with a broken stem."[19]

Together with Mother Shipp she did everything for him, Mother Shipp with her years of experience and Ellis "with all the intensity of a true mother love."[20] Even in her grief Ellis was cognizant of inner forces and causes: "But, alas, we knew not the intricate mysteries of disease nor the blessed gift of healing."[21] This realization gave her grief power that would rise to the surface later in life.

In December Willie died. Milford was not with her. How could she bear such pain without him there? Without his beautiful voice, his eloquent speech to unfold the truths which could heal her spirit? She was pregnant again, which made things just that much harder. Little Bard, her firstborn, was not quite two. In his innocent, angelic way he was her comfort.

> How could I lie me down desolate and without peace and hope with such a precious form in my arms, such precious little hands to grasp my own, to stroke my drooping head, to dry my tears, to lisp in childish tone, "Mama, don't you cry."[22]

It helped Ellis through this time, in the early hours, the quiet before the rest of the world was awake, to work on plans for self-improvement. "The humble prayer, the morning air, the thoughts I gleaned from books—all were jewels rare, becoming bulwarks of defense against all tendency to lose self-control, to even think or say or act unjustly."[23]

In May when the earth was renewing itself, when beauty brought hope and reason for going on, her third little son, Richard Asbury, was born. Nine days later Milford left for a mission to England. Ellis was still not well, but she summoned her courage, happy that one so capable as Milford had opportunity to preach the gospel and bless the lives of others. She felt that she could willingly endure anything the Lord required.

Although they were rich in faith they were poor in worldly means. Ellis, however, was handy with a needle. She did fancy sewing for others. And she had her cow—her cow and her orchard, both wedding gifts from her father.

> My independent nature felt so glad to be self-sustaining, for I resolved to lean as far as mortal could upon myself and trust in God to pave the way to avenues whereby our daily needs could be honorably met.[24]

This philosophy reflects Brigham Young's influence upon her. He taught and practiced a practical cooperation between God and man:

> My faith does not lead me to think the Lord will provide us with roast pigs, bread already buttered, etc.—He will give us the ability to raise the grain, to obtain the fruits, to make the habitation.—Implied faith and confidence in God is for you and me to do everything we can to sustain and preserve ourselves. Instead of searching after what the Lord is going to do for us, let us inquire what we can do ourselves. My faith is, when we have done all we can, then the Lord is under obligation, and will not disappoint the faithful; He will perform the rest.[25]

While Ellis was busy contriving ways to support herself and the children, Milford was having some challenging experiences of his own. En route to New York he stopped off to visit his birthplace, Edinburgh, Indiana. He met and visited with several old friends. When they learned he was on his way to fill a mission for his church in England, they offered to hire a church where he could preach a sermon on Mormonism.

The suggestion was spontaneous and somewhat naive. None of the ministers would allow him to occupy their pulpits. The fairgrounds were obtained instead. An unprecidented crowd, nearly two thousand, came to hear the Mormon preach. All of the ministers were there, more hostile than curious. But "he held his listeners spellbound while he taught them the first principles of the gospel. He felt his voice failing and when he looked at the clock found he had talked for an hour and a half. He closed the meeting, but the audience clamored for more. The newspaper in Franklin, a nearby settlement, made this comment, 'Mr. Shipp is on his way to Europe for three years and expects to make thousands of converts to the Mormon cause. Better that he should be drowned in the depths of the sea.' "[26]

In the autumn Ellis spent some time in Pleasant Grove, staying with her beloved grandparents and garnering the apples and peaches from her orchards. While her babies played on a quilt spread over the leaves, she climbed the tall, rickety ladder and picked the ripe fruit, which she would later dry and preserve.

Near this time William Hawley built a hotel in Pleasant Grove. Both he and his wife Ellis remembered fondly the days at their Canadian Inn. The Hawley House was the first hotel the city boasted. Built of soft rock, the center part was two stories high, the east and west wings one and a half stories. The old couple had been nurturing people, taking strangers in for as long as anyone who knew them could remember; it was natural for them to embark upon such a venture.

Spring 1871 rolled around. Milford had been gone nearly two years. Ellis celebrated her fifth wedding anniversary without him, but with a grateful heart for this "companion of her inner soul."[27] She was teaching school at this time in the Eleventh Ward adobe meetinghouse, and keeping active in both the Relief Society and Retrenchment organizations.

When Sister Hoge was released as secretary of their ward Relief Society, Bishop McRae called Ellis to fill her place. He and his counselors felt, since her duties would be quite numerous and time-consuming, that she ought to receive some remuneration, but Ellis refused.

"It is little I have done for this kingdom," she told them, "and I am thankful and feel it an honor and privilege to do good in the kingdom." She was later to confide in her journal, "I feel weak, but I will rely on my Heavenly Father, for I know He will bless my feeble efforts, for He has said, 'Unto thy day, thy strength shall be.' "[28]

Milford wrote throughout the long months, instructing his wives, sometimes chastising them. "Milford thinks that we do not write as frequently or explicitly as we might, so I must hasten and write a good letter, one that will redeem myself from past remissness. I do desire to write good letters, something that will cheer and comfort him in his absence from home and its associations, and encourage him in his labors."[29]

With or without what he considered proper sustenance, Milford was doing well on his mission. He had preached in places where no Mormon Elders had been admitted, and his golden tongue won many converts and much good will for the Church. He was sustained as president of the Leeds Conference and held that position until his release.

There were, naturally, difficult days for Ellis, when the cares of life pressed in on her sensitive soul.

> I have just completed my morning's work and have been resting about ten minutes, the longest respite I have had for weeks. With my school and the numerous other duties I have to perform, my time is completely monopolized. Not only my time but my thoughts and my mind are necessarily occupied with the cares of everyday life, this temporal existence that requires so much flour and potatoes for its sustenance.
>
> I do not wish to complain, but I sometimes feel sorrowful that I have no more time for meditation and reflection, that I cannot study and glean truths from the many great works that are lying so profusely around me. I do desire knowledge![30]

Hand in hand with her desire for self-improvement was her fervent desire to be a good, wise mother.

> This morning I arose at four, hoed in the garden till five, then returned to my room and beside the bed where my two darlings sleep, I fell upon my knees to pour forth some of the deepest desires of my soul. I do desire to be wise, that I may do some good in the world, that I may perform faithfully a mother's part to the jewels entrusted to my care. How wise a mother should be, for oh, how much does the weal or woe of the child depend upon her training![31]

One particular Friday Ellis returned from school "weary and despondent."[32] She had a severe headache; the children had been harder than usual to manage. Maggie, seeing her mood, took her gently into the parlor and directed her gaze to the mantlepiece where a portrait of Milford rested. Ellis was too moved with deep emotion to speak. She took the picture and a letter that had just arrived in the mail and retired to her room, where she could lie on her bed and weep with no one to see. It was joy to see this semblance of Milford before her, but sad that the original was gone from her now, not there to love and comfort and sustain her.

It was springtime, though, and soon a letter arrived with the joyous news that Milford would be returning—in only three weeks time! There were days of happy preparation and anxious longing, and prayers offered for his safe return.

On July 12, 1861, Milford arrived home, after an absence of just over two years. Ellis's joy and gratitude were complete. She spent Pioneer Day, July 24, with him, basking again in his love and counsel. It seemed that often their conversation centered on spiritual, eternal themes. Even in this holiday setting Milford talked "principle," marking out "the course we should take to gain an exaltation, that in this life we must lay a foundation, extensive, firm, and steadfast, that cannot be overthrown."[33]

Milford brought an English family back with him, a family he had converted to the gospel, who in turn had cared for him during a serious illness. Ellis felt very grateful to the Hillsteads for being "instruments in the hand of God in preserving his life."[34]

"Oh, should I not feel grateful for their kindness," she wrote in her journal. "O, Father in heaven, bless them and I pray thee, to give into my hands power to recompense them for their many kind and noble services unto one who was far away from kindred, friends, and home."[35]

Ellis was still struggling with the challenges of living plural marriage. Shortly after Milford's return there was some small problem concerning discipline of the children. Ellis recorded how she prayed alone in her room, asking that the pure spirit of God might rest in her heart. While still praying she heard Maggie's voice calling. She concluded her prayer and went upstairs to see what Maggie wanted.

She found her in tears, unable to speak. Gently Ellis slipped her arm around her waist and waited until Maggie was calm enough to explain. It really was a little matter. She had asked Milford not to allow Ellis to read a letter he had written to both his wives concerning some trouble with little Bard, Ellis's oldest son. He had denied her request and now she wondered if Ellis would also refuse.

All the sympathy in Ellis's nature was aroused. She answered, "Maggie, I have no desire to read it whatever. No, I will not read it." She later recorded, "For, oh, I feel humble. I wish to forgive and forget, as I wish to have my weaknesses forgiven and forgotten. I truly believe our embraces linked our hearts in an indissolvable union. Maggie and I have lived together for years — our aims, desires, thoughts, and interests have been the same, and although there has been an occasional discord in our feelings, I truly believe the holy relationship existing between us causes us to feel a sympathy and love for each other that two souls under other circumstances could never experience. We know each other's faults and we know each other's virtues and, oh, I pray fervently that we may be patient and charitable — praise and emulate the virtues, and forget the errors."[36]

When Ellis went downstairs Milford was just going out. But he took the letter from his pocket and offered it to her. She told him she did not wish to read it. "There is really little in it," he replied, "to cause trouble." Such family disturbances worried Milford. It was clear to Ellis that he wanted nothing more than peace and union in his family, that digression from that standard disturbed him deeply.

Ellis vowed to do all she could to provide him with his ideal. She was twenty-four years old at this time, but mature beyond her years and strongly determined to attain an almost impossible ideal, to pull it down and make it serve her on a practical day-to-day level.

The same evening Maggie wrote an entry in Ellis's journal, encouraged by her sister-wife's magnanimity, to express for the first time some of her own deepest emotions:

> Ellis — there is a desire to write a few words in your journal. Ellis, there are few people who know each other as we do. Our situation and circumstances have been peculiarly adapted to the searching out and becoming almost perfectly acquainted with each other. Trivial affairs have occurred to excite our impatience, and we have forgotten the noble virtues that reside within us.
>
> Nearly four years we have been "married" and I have never conferred any depth of affection or been at all demonstrative. But for once I let you gaze into my soul. Polygamy is from God — it is pure — and although my mind is occasionally clouded, yet generally the principle appears clear and practicable. Ellis, there is no woman

that I ever met (I will not except any) with whom I would rather be connected. Oh, sister dear, I appreciate your noble soul, wise judgment, and sympathetic heart. My love is genuine and I truly believe it will exist throughout the eternities. I desire your love, your interest, your watchful care, and all that I can offer in the world is yours.

I tell you, principle is the great necessity. 'Tis the safest platform. Oh, let us draw near to each other, let us continue to pray together, be determined to exercise charity and forbearance. My heart is sick and my thoughts unmingled, but you know that my desires are earnest, humble, and holy.   Maggie Shipp[37]

With such humility and determination these two noble women struggled to overcome and succeed.

In September Ellis left for Pleasant Grove to stay with her grandparents and attend to her orchard. But this time there was an important difference. She left her little sons behind. She had never been separated from her children, even for a single night. But Milford desired her to leave them and she bowed before what she considered his greater wisdom. "I have a great desire," she recorded at this time, "to overcome all the weak points of my nature, to have no feelings that I cannot control by the force and power of my will."[38]

The impulses were there—the beginnings of understanding. But she could not know the wisdom of what she desired and what she did. All this was only preparation for the colossal experiences that waited ahead. She would need to discipline her motherly feelings for the real partings she was soon to face. The "force and power" of her will would rise to the foreground and make it possible for her to accomplish deeds beyond her wildest dreams and imaginings.

She was in Pleasant Grove several weeks and while she was there Milford paid her a hasty visit, bringing the children, filling her empty cup with unexpected joy. Perhaps he felt it was the least he could do for her. She was pregnant again and not really well, and he had plans that did not sit too well with her. On October 23 he married another wife—Elizabeth, daughter of the English family he had baptized. In November, home from Battle Creek, Ellis was able to record in her journal:

I do not allow myself to become low-spirited. I have trusted in my Heavenly Father and He has blessed me. I know there is but one way to be happy in polygamy and that is to keep burning in our hearts the spirit of God.[39]

Yet in February 1873 she made a poignant entry, referring back to the words she had written at Milford's return concerning her feelings of gratitude to the Hillsteads: "I pray thee to give into my hands power to recompense them for their many kind and noble services. . . ." February 17 she wrote: "When I made this solemn, earnest request of my Heavenly Father I did not realize in what way my prayer would be granted. For a year and a half Elizabeth Hillstead has been Milford's wife and I feel to strive with all my might and power to be kind, considerate, and charitable."[40]

The year ticked to an inevitable ending. Ellis, rather than reviewing her successes, berated herself in her usual fashion for the faults, the weaknesses she had failed to control. Yet she was full of resolves for the new year before her:

> January 1, 1872: I begin upon a new page and upon a new year. How uncertain is life! I know not what circumstance will cause me to write upon these pages—nor do I know what my actions will be in the days of the year to come. It appears today that circumstance is the ruling power.
>
> This morning I arose at four—with hopes high and determination strong. I began my studies with zeal, animated by the fond desires of making myself a companion for my husband—this was not all—for I desired to be kind, generous, and noble, to commit no action, have no thoughts but that God would approbate, to ever be patient and enduring and never cause a cloud to mar the sunshine of our home.
>
> Perhaps I was too enthusiastic, for scarcely had we exchanged the greetings of the day when I gave utterance to words that caused gloom in the household and sorrow in my heart. The children had committed some mischief—their father punished them. Bard was in the blame—I could not see why he should always be blamed. I thought one of the others was mostly at fault—and said so. Milford thought I was criticizing him and did not want Bard punished, and thus I brought discord where I had hoped to have joy, peace, and happiness.
>
> Oh, why did I not have more judgment—why could I not restrain those words that were the outflowings of a mother's sensitive heart. Milford blames me and doubtless ever will in this life, but with the aid of my Heavenly Father I will endeavor never to give

expression to anything that will have the least semblance of opposition to his actions or wishes. For as I live upon the earth I wish to be
a good and true wife and mother. . . .[41]

Her sincerity could move the stoniest heart to tears. Ellis was
plagued by her constant failing to reach her ideal, and even more
by any displeasure she caused her husband. Milford was very manipulative in his relationships with others; Ellis, because of the
depth of her love and devotion for him, was especially susceptible
to his manipulative tendencies. In the autobiography she wrote in
her later years she gave expression to a hard-won insight:

> Many, many years of our wedded life had passed ere I could
> ever believe it possible for him to make one mistake, and always, if
> ever one little mistake was made to cause a ruffled feeling, I *ever
> blamed myself.* And how I grieved over that one sad discovery! Poor
> blind child that I was. I should have known that every mortal is but
> human, and in this earthly probation we cannot expect perfection.
> We should not, for sooner or later we will be disillusioned.[42]

January seemed destined to be a most difficult month, one
that would try all her high resolves in a dozen ways. She was still
following her plan of early rising, studying on her own from four
till seven. Milford was immersed in his own studies, trying to gain
a proficiency in law. He had fitted up Maggie's room for his use;
Ellis hardly saw him. She tried to become so involved in her own
work that she didn't miss him. She called this his "one last great
effort to arrive at greatness and eminence,"[43] revealing that she
knew how important it was to him.

As early as this Ellis was studying the work of Dr. Gunn, re-
cording that she deemed it "the duty of every mother to understand perfectly the laws of health."[44] If she spent an occasional half
hour alone with Milford she was happy — or tried to feel as contented as she could.

January 7 was a Sunday. At two o'clock in the afternoon Ellis
took her little boys, Bard and Richie, and along with Milford and
Maggie went to church. The building was too crowded for them to
find seats, so she left with the children, though apparently Milford
and Maggie stayed. She walked toward home, but little Richie
grew tired, so when she reached the tall, inviting gate of the Bee-

hive House she decided to go in and visit Sister Lucy and rest the children awhile.

She sat down in the familiar front parlor, enjoying the elegant peace that surrounded her there. They were no sooner settled than Brigham himself walked in. He greeted her with warmth and kindness. It was the Sabbath — surely his precious hours were marked for something. But for a wonderful half hour he sat with her, doing little things to amuse the children, making her feel remarkably relaxed and accepted.

As she rose to leave he caught her gaze and his blue eyes held hers, deep and guileless, sincere as a child's. He said, and his voice was tender with feeling, "Peace be unto you."[45] The words entered Ellis's heart like a shaft of warm light. She later recorded: "Methinks if ever there was a heavenly look in man it can be seen in his countenance."[46]

The same evening she attended a meeting where Milford spoke and was thrilled to note the rapt attention of the audience, and to feel the beauty and power in his words. It was what she had needed — a day of feasting. It encouraged her to redouble her efforts to do all that was right.

Remembering that Ellis was pregnant with her fourth child and had the care of two little ones as well as the running of a household, it is enlightening to read an example of her daily routine. This was recorded under the date of January 8, 1872:

> Rise at four in the morning, dress, make a fire, wash in cold water, comb my hair, clean my teeth. Write a few lines in my journal, write a letter to grandmother. Read a chapter in Dr. Gunn on health. Read a few extracts from Johnson. Dress the children, make bed, sweep, dust, and prepare my room for the breakfast table. Breakfast at nine.
>
> Sew on the machine until three — dinner hour. After dinner call on Sister Jones, who is sick. Wash and prepare the children for bed; from six till eight knit or do some other light work. Review my actions for the day — offer my devotions to heaven, and retire at nine.[47]

The spirit was willing, but the flesh was a thorn in her side. There were days she felt too unwell to keep going. Once or twice she was forced to take to her bed; she then felt very much like giving up. Often she gave way to frustrated tears, then would remind herself that she must not succumb to bodily aches and pains. There were too many important things to be done. She must be more "assiduous in my efforts to govern and control my children, more constant and regular with Bard's lessons, more economical with my time and more faithful in my prayers."[48] And, as if that wasn't enough, she added more items: "Study philosophy, revive my poetical inclinations, cultivate good language and conversational powers, finish reading the Book of Mormon."[49]

Milford had been teaching his wives for years a course to pursue "that will place her (the wife) upon the pinnacle of eminence in her husband's affections and esteem."[50] Ellis tried with all her power to live it, to incorporate his instructions into her daily routine. But these days were hard and discouraging for her. There were three wives and several children in one small household, as well as a husband working at home who demanded quiet. She was pregnant and sick and under strain. It seemed at times Milford didn't appreciate her efforts, nor realize all she had to contend with. She wrote, with a spirit of melancholy, "I will try and be patient and uncomplaining and hope for better days—and for encouragement." She lived for Milford's encouragement and praise. "Often," she confided to her journal, "the clouds look dark and my heart feels like it would break."[51]

She was approaching her twenty-fifth birthday. Maybe she *was* feeling a little sorry for herself. One night, when she was alone with Milford, she succumbed to the temptation to complain, and confided some of her complaints to him—even directing one or two pointedly at him.

She accused him of being somewhat partial, of withholding the comfort that a look or word of encouragement would contain. Milford listened, his solemn brown eyes upon her. He made no reply, but drew out a paper and said he would read something that would prove how mistaken she was.

He referred to a tribute he had written for her birthday—full of tender love and praise, speaking of Ellis's patience and forbearance, reminiscing about the early days when she, his "sunshine," had come to his rescue and brought hope and purpose back to his life again. Each word was like a shaft of pain through her.

"Oh, had I but waited two days later!" she lamented in anguish. "It would have been to me the richest, most priceless boon my heart could crave, but to hear it under such circumstances filled my heart with sorrow the most keen, and regret most poignant and unavailable."[52]

She reached out her hand for the paper, knowing she didn't fully deserve the praise, but longing for it. Milford, still gazing at her, crushed the paper in his hand "as if by the act he would obliterate every word it contained, and that he was free from any delusions he might have labored under regarding my uncomplaining nobleness."[53]

Ellis was as crushed as the crumpled missive. "This is the most severe and cutting reproof I ever had from my husband," she recorded. What could she do to regain the thing she most valued — "the respect and esteem of Milford"?[54]

The next day she was still depressed and felt "as keenly as ever the depth of my humiliation and regret. But by the aid of a kind and merciful Father I will regain what I have apparently lost."[55] Milford's way of punishing an offender was to withhold himself. This was torture to Ellis, who could never bring herself to find fault with him, but added her own condemnation to his, and lived in the misery of self-deprecation.

When her birthday arrived she continued the process, going over the years of her life with a fine-tooth comb, analyzing, tearing apart, judging herself harshly.

> Twenty-five years ago as the sun came over the hill I was born. Yes, God placed me upon this earth to accomplish some purpose. Twenty-five years — a quarter of a century — has elapsed. And what are my accomplishments? A very few. There are very few of my weaknesses that I have brought into subjection — but few of my talents that I have cultivated — and I feel but little good I have done.[56]

Perhaps it is key that at least she said, "God placed me upon this earth to accomplish some purpose." She still felt there was something for her to do, something above and beyond the ordinary.

"O, what might not be accomplished?" she pondered, harking back to her cherished memories of her mother, which moved her to respond, "With her advice and instruction and her most perfect example (and I never saw one to excel it) oh, should I not be a good and noble woman?"[57]

The day she had so dreaded turned out to be pleasant. Maggie, Lizzie, and several of her friends gave her thoughtful presents. But that wasn't the real source of her joy. Milford's tribute? He had not really destroyed it. The period of penance was through. He presented it to her, moving her to respond, "Oh, what is purer and nobler than the love that exists between a true husband and wife, those who live for each other and for heaven?"[58]

Fear and sickness had begun to seem part of Ellis's life. In February both her boys were ill. Little Bard, with childlike faith, told his mother that Richie would be well in the morning because Papa was going to pray for him tonight. The boys did get well, in time for the birth of her baby on April 8, 1872. A daughter—at last she was blessed with a daughter! But she was not well, nor was the baby. Her anxiety was worse to bear than her physical pain.

On May 1 she went for a ride with Sister Freeze, weak still, but much encouraged by the beauty and sunlight. May 5, 1872, was her sixth wedding anniversary. Milford preached at the Seventh Ward, then returned home and blessed her baby girl, giving her the name of Anna—"for my dear sainted mother."[59] Then the ups and downs of life began again.

Milford was called out of town, to Beaver. Ellis struggled with the void she felt when he wasn't there. Little Richie had his third birthday. She rose at five to pull weeds and feed chickens, visited a Sister Dunfords who was "in polygamy" but in reality knew little of it, surrounded with comforts and luxuries, living *alone*. She visited Brigham and his family, who asked questions curiously, wondering how they all lived together in peace, thinking that women who could raise children together in such circumstances must be saints.

Ellis agreed and the point made her, as usual, begin to ponder. "Methinks her glory (speaking of women like Sister Dunfords) will not be equal that of the poor woman who has few of this world's goods, but has proven herself a true Latter-day Saint by bearing patiently the trials of polygamy."[60]

Milford returned safely, Ellis was once more happy. But several days later she innocently offended him. "My spirits are depressed," she recorded. "My only comfort is that I intended no wrong. I feel to 'trust in God and do the right.' But oh, it is hard to feel that we have the displeasure of our dearest friends. That a friend whose interests are dearer to us than life deems us careless and inconsiderate. How strange that a single unwise act in a friend will cause us to forget many kind, noble, and generous deeds of former years."[61]

Milford's rejection, though temporary, wounded her deeply and unconsciously did much to feed her low self-image and the self-defeating criticism she inflicted upon herself.

Two weeks later a Retrenchment ball was held. Ellis read here an essay she had written on retrenchment. It pleased her husband — and that was what she most desired. "He encourages me to cultivate my talents," she wrote, "to study, write, and improve every moment of time, and he says he thinks I will be enabled to do good in the world."[62]

She clung to those words as one would cling to a lifeline, wanting desperately to believe them, strengthened by the fact that Milford thought they were true.

In spite of all her protestations to the contrary, plural marriage was wrenchingly difficult for Ellis. In early August she was baptized for four young women who had died as innocent maids; she records their names as Kate, Martha, Marie, and Margaret Tower. Then she entered the Endowment House and with Milford went through the sacred ordinance of sealing them to Milford in their behalf.

"I feel that I am greatly blessed," she recorded, "and I desire most fervently to do worthy of the glorious blessings and privileges that I possess."[63]

But Milford was to take another earthly wife, Mary Smith Coteral, on February 10, 1873. On August 10 Ellis recorded her feelings:

> My prayer is this morning that I may overcome my selfishness and jealousy, especially with my husband's attention. May I ever appreciate any attention or kindness I may receive. But oh, may these longings and cravings for his society and attention cease — more particularly when it is another's right to possess them.[64]

It seems her greatest, or only, fault was that she loved too well. Few men have enjoyed such overwhelming devotion from a woman as sensitive, feminine, and intelligent as Ellis.

Milford's thirty-seventh birthday was approaching. Ellis was struggling with poor health at the time, suffering greatly, sometimes lying in bed for several days, fighting the constant threat of discouragement. "Without health there is no usefulness," she wrote, "and without usefulness, no happiness."[65] Yet there were times she had a strong, peaceful feeling. And to whom did she attribute this happy state?

> It is because Milford — our husband — is the man he is; because he is so kind and generous, so noble, chaste, and pure, and by his advice, counsels, and exemplary course leads his family in the path of truth and righteousness.[66]

On March 1 all four wives — Ellis, Maggie, Lizzie and Mary — went to the photograph gallery and had their picture taken as a present for Milford's birthday. Ellis wrote a poem to go with the picture. Their faces look out at us now: Ellis — wide-eyed and serious, achingly lovely in a sensitive yet spirited way; Maggie — with rich, dark ringlets, a long, oval face both intelligent and pretty; Lizzie — her dark eyes looking somewhat wild and rebellious, her small face attractive and interesting; and Mary — lighter haired, somewhat chubby, with plain, more gentle features, her round face holding an expression that is almost shy. They placed the picture and poem under his plate at breakfast. "We all feel to say," Ellis wrote, "God bless our Bard, (Milford) and may he see many returns of the day."[67]

That same month Ellis became quite ill again. Lizzie stayed with her when the others went out, taking tender care of her, "a kindness," Ellis said, "that I will not soon forget."[68] Milford administered to her and it made a difference. She recorded in her journal, "He pronounced great things upon my head."[69] Milford's faith in what she was capable of still persisted.

On April 1 Lizzie's little Carl died, reopening the only partially healed wound of her own loss of Willie. On April 10 Brigham came to dinner, an honor that Ellis fully appreciated.

Even at that time Ellis often consulted Brigham. She still enjoyed that somewhat intimate relationship and could turn to him for personal counsel and aid.

On Sunday, April 20, Mother Shipp came to visit and upbraided Ellis for not defending Flora to Brigham Young. Apparently there was some trouble between her daughter, Flora, and her husband, Theodor. Mother Shipp thought Ellis should have vindicated Flora by telling more of Theodor's faults. The quality Ellis displayed as a girl when she defended the boy being punished by the schoolmaster came to the fore in her reply to Milford's mother:

> I am sorry that they feel so, but I did what I thought was my duty. I spoke of Flora — extolled her virtues as a wife and as a faithful Saint — but as for Theodor, I said nothing — and that is why they censure me.
>
> President Young is a man of strong prejudices. When he once forms an opinion it is hard to change him, almost an impossibility, and I have seen so many suffer from the effects of reports made to him that it makes me consider before I say anything derrogatory of any person's character. I know I feel if a person errs — if we can do nothing to reclaim him, we should at least not push him down.[70]

Hadn't she — hadn't they all — seen Milford himself suffer so? Not only is her native charity displayed here, but the extent of her understanding of Brigham Young and how to handle him on a human, personal level.

Spring came, but Ellis was still despondent:

> Milford and Lizzie have gone to her mother's to supper. Maggie has gone home with Mother Shipp. Mary is sick upstairs — her

mother is with her. Blessed girl, *her mother is with her.* I feel discouraged. I am at a loss what to do with my children, they are so wild,
so ungovernable. I desire to be a good mother, but it seems I lack
the government and judgment. How it pains me as I write it, to
think I have not power to govern my little ones. Oh, could they
but realize the love, the all-absorbing feelings of a mother's heart,
they could at least repay her with obedience, but I know the defi-
ciency must lie in the training and government of the child—but
when one is weakened with sickness and pain, what can she do?[71]

Her seventh wedding anniversary arrived. The gloom she had
felt subsided and hope washed over her like the rays of the warm
May sunlight. What was the cause of this change of feelings?

Oh, it is the words, the cheering, strengthening words of my
husband. I believe my devotion to him is the most pure and sincere
and I feel to sustain him by faith, prayers, and works. He is a kind
and noble husband. I realize the prayer I offered seven years ago has
not been unavailing, that my Father has blessed me in the election I
made. He has been to me all that woman could desire.[72]

Ellis, due to her poor health, was not making the difficult trip
to Arizona, where Milford had been called to serve a brief mission.
Milford wished to leave Lizzie with her, and Ellis agreed, though
this had not been her desire. On a morning of rain and gloom the
family departed, taking little Bard with them, leaving Ellis and
Lizzie behind. It rained all day long. In the evening Lizzie found a
beautiful box from Mary in her drawer, and Ellis discovered a
brooch left by Maggie. The thoughtful little gifts helped dispel
the gloom.

On May 27 she celebrated Richard's fourth birthday. Grandmother Hawley and Ellis's sister were both there and her joy—her
rich, emotional joy—seemed overflowing. Thoughts of the magnitude of motherhood might nearly overwhelm her, but they held
power to sustain Ellis as well. She recorded here, as she did so
often, many of her feelings about that most sacred office. In June, a
few weeks later, she said: "I think my desires for health and long
life were never so strong, for my earthly work is but just begun. I
know that in that blest abode there is no more sorrow, no more
pain, but I would rather live—I am willing to endure the sufferings
of this life if I can but fill my mission in usefullness."[73]

In July she visited Pleasant Grove, was strengthened by the associations there, but appalled by the carelessness and neglect of many of the people.

> To see women drinking tea and coffee and opposing polygamy. Men, who should set the example to their families, using tobacco, drinking whiskey, swearing, and speaking of the authorities in the vilest terms. What wonder is it that children walk in the same path. Oh, why do not this people live up to their privileges?[74]

It was this same summer that Eliza R. Snow first approached Ellis with the idea of studying medicine. Much was being said about the subject at the time. Ellis had attended the Retrenchment classes, directed by Sarah Kimball, on the subject of physiology. Sister Snow knew of her interest in the field and also had some appreciation of the qualities Ellis had to offer. Eliza reminded her that it was Brigham's desire to see women educate themselves in this field, and believed she would be one to step out in this direction.

"I thought it would be what I would love and delight in, if this knowledge could be obtained here," Ellis confided. "But the thought of leaving home and loved ones overwhelmed me and swept from me even the possibility of making the attempt."[75]

Near the end of July her family returned and little Bard was restored to her, healthy and happy. A few quiet, happy weeks followed—the last she was to enjoy for a long time. During this period she penned some of her feelings about love and the man-woman relationship.

> Man in seeking a wife desires a helpmeet, a companion in every sense of the word—one who will bear with pleasure and joy the cares of maternity for the sake of adding to his glory. Woman gives her hand, her heart, her all to her husband, *she gives herself*. The apex of her hopes is one whom she can love and honor as her head, one who is wise and judicious and is governed, and governs, by the pure principles of the gospel.[76]

Ellis was one whose actions were greatly influenced by her principles. Her independent spirit might have asserted itself very differently in our day. But she was, after all, a product of her own time. She has left many thrilling statements on principle, one of the most magnificent being the following:

> *If,* in the eternal plan, woman should be led, it should be a
> capable leadership. My ideal of the union of the sexes I had found
> in the blessed union of my parents, for they were indeed "two souls
> with but one single heart; two hearts that beat as one." Never in
> their lives was there the arrogance of domination. How I praise the
> Eternal Father for this sublime example, this pattern for carrying on
> life's purposes, our Creator's sacred command for mortal companion-
> ship, a union divine which all should understand lasts throughout all
> the eternities of time.
>
> What a wretched thought to believe that marriage is to last but
> a week, a year, or even to end with death. Such sacred companion-
> ship is for time and all eternity, for all the mortal and immortal days
> of our existence.[77]

She might feel that she fell short of her parents' ideal. Milford
might even fall short, though Ellis could not see it. But what she
could see she faced squarely, with courage and love. She could see
her duty and she would not shirk it. She could see the glowing promise that at last would be hers when this earth life was through.
She kept her eye on the shining goal and if she faltered, it was only
from human weakness, never from lack of purpose or desire.

The last day of September 1873, little Anna died. "Her bright
spirit departed, leaving that beloved form — so fair and lovely in
life — cold, cold and motionless."[78] For eighteen months she had
been a bright gem, a delight to her mother. Although she had been
sick for nearly two months, Ellis had never anticipated that Anna
would die.

"Oh, I thought He would spare her — my faith was so great
and so strong. Never for a moment did I think she would be taken
away till I saw death upon her. Ah, and even then I felt that nothing is impossible with God, and I believed it was His will to let her
live upon the earth and accomplish the great work that I, in my
solicitude, had planned for my treasure."[79]

Her loss was too much for Ellis's sensitivities. It threw her into
a period of spiritual anguish and physical illness. Milford had been
making arrangements for some time to take his entire family south
on a trip. He continued with the plans, thinking the change might
be good for Ellis. He even sent her ahead of the others so that she

might rest and visit and renew herself with her father and his family in Mount Pleasant.

But nothing worked to dispel Anna's image from her mind. Every person, every place stirred memories of her. Ellis tried to say, "Thy will, not mine be done." She tried to remember that Anna was not really lost to her. But her affection had been too deep to shake off so quickly.

In November at her father's house she was still too weak to get out of bed or walk about. The holidays approached and she seemed little better. Maggie's birthday was December 17. She wrote a few lines, but they didn't please her. She didn't think them worthy for Maggie to see. On December 18 she, Milford, Lizzie, and her boys went to North Bend where Milford was to speak. In the congregation Ellis noticed a woman near her holding a baby, and thoughts of Anna swept through her with fresh heartache and pain.

> I envied not the woman her happiness, but the picture reminded me of my darling, of my sad loss.

> > When I see a happy mother
> > With her infant on her knee,
> > Oh, 'tis hard my grief to smother,
> > For no sweet babe smiles on me.
> > No bright eyes beam upon me,
> > With their innocent pure light,
> > They're beaming now in heaven,
> > Far from my loving sight.
> > No sweet voice says, "My Mama,"
> > No soft hand on my brow
> > To still its weary throbbing,
> > I have no Anna now.

> Oh, sweet darling Anna, how Mama misses thee! Never, never can I forget the look from those eyes when they saw tears in mine, and that sweet face rayed with a look of heaven, to kiss away my tears. Oh, why did I weep when I had thee, sweet babe?[80]

Christmas Day Ellis had the quiet pleasure of seeing her Bard — the affectionate name she and the other wives called him — with his entire family partake of a feast beneath her father's roof. In the afternoon they all took a sleigh ride in the clean, bracing winter air. In the evening they sang old home songs together. A little peace started seeping into her heart.

In January 1874 Ellis turned twenty-seven years old. That same month William Hawley was rebaptized. Elder Orson Hyde the Apostle came from his home in Sanpete and appeared unexpectedly at the Hawley House. He grasped his old friend warmly by the hand and said simply, "Brother Hawley, I've come to baptize you."

William heartily answered, "All right, I'm ready."[81]

His daughter, Sarah Ellis, has left a lively account of the event:

> It was mid-January and bitterly cold, so that the pond in the fields halfway to the lake—which was the nearest available place—was covered by eight inches of ice. Men were sent to cut the ice away, my brother Vance being one of them. Then the wagon box was filled with straw and warm quilts and blankets and hot bricks. They made the trip through the fields with the rheumatic old man of seventy-one and baptized him in that icy water, which was a heroic thing for several people, and then rode back in their wet clothes, but he was wrapped snuggly in warm bedding so that he suffered no ill effects from the icy plunge. Oh, were we happy.[82]

Ellis recorded the event in her journal. "Just heard the news that my grandfather had been baptized into this Church—Oh, how thankful I am! My heart is full of gratitude that He has answered this oft-repeated prayer."[83]

Ellis stayed in Mount Pleasant several weeks longer. At times, as her strength returned, she felt light and hopeful. At times the pain and fear would overtake her.

> For a time last night I was very sick. Never did I have such strange sensations. For a moment, but only for a moment, I felt that life was departing.[84]

And her heart was still very tender and saddened. "My heart," she wrote, "is too susceptible of sorrow. It breaks down beneath a burden that some would carry with ease."[85]

But this very quality, which she deemed a weakness, helped enable her to fulfill the magnificent promise of her life.

Milford was gone on business trips during much of this period, and Ellis missed him with her usual intensity.

On March 12, bright and early, they left for Salt Lake. Milford had returned and at last was taking her home. It was a difficult trip, with a severe storm to endure as well as the usual strain and fatigue of travel. But Ellis was too delighted to care.

The end of the month found her struggling to regain her health, trying to follow Milford's admonitions. "Milford wishes me to not think or worry about the work, but make myself contented that I may the sooner regain my strength. May heaven help me to remember his words."[86]

In the summer Milford was busy with a new project, one that had been very close to his heart for some time. In the *Deseret News* of July 3, 1874, the following notice was published:

> Mr. M.B. Shipp has completed his arrangements in the 13th Ward for entering upon the fruit and vegetable canning business, and expects to commence upon peas and corn on Monday. He has had a suitable furnace constructed and also boilers in which the fruit or vegetables are to be heated preparatory to canning. Mr. Shipp is confident that he can compete successfully in the point of price and quality with importations in the line, and it is hoped he will be able to do so; we see no reason why he shouldn't.[87]

Milford personally supervised the various processes, and by August had twenty-five to thirty men working for him. The quality of his fruit was unsurpassed. The cans he used were made of substantial double tin and would hold from two to two and a-half pounds. It was an exciting enterprise for the entire family.

On September 22, 1874, Ellis's fourth son, Burt Reynolds, was born. She wrote: "God gave me another precious treasure of heaven."[88] But just over two weeks later, on October 8, she recorded: "Milford was called on a mission to the States. How strange it is that he should be separated from us so much—but I will never murmur when I know that it is for the redemption of souls he labors."[89]

The mission was of only short duration, but it played havoc with Milford's business concerns. February 1875 sees him moving all of his family, with the exception of Ellis, into a house in the

Thirteenth Ward where his canning establishment was located. March 5 he moved them back home again. As Ellis stated, "the business relations between himself and father are dissolving. Milford feels discouraged, but I think all will turn out right."[90]

Father and son had been partners in the canning business. Ellis trusted that God would overrule all things for their good and expressed her desire that she might be an instrument in His hands, that the light and joy of her own heart might comfort her husband. It was always her wish to lift and lighten those around her, but above all to be a blessing to Milford, to prove worthy of his faith and love.

By the spring of 1875 Ellis had her life back in some semblance of order again. Her health was better than it had been for a long time. She was involved in activities that made her feel useful and progressive. On April 18 Milford came home from the Sugar House Ward with unexpected news. He had bought a little farm! It was only ten acres, but it sported a house and a splendid orchard and was reasonably priced at twelve hundred dollars. The boys were ecstatic, but the wives all hesitated. Who wanted to go out so far to live?

Ellis was the first to volunteer. She felt the fresh air and surroundings would be good for her sons, and perhaps the peace would be good for her own spirit. Mary said she, too, would go and that pleased Ellis. That same afternoon they drove the two and a half miles to see it. In addition to orchard and fields there was a small grove of cottonwood trees which sheltered a spring of the clearest, coldest water Ellis ever had tasted.

April and May were strenuous months, but very productive. They whitewashed and cleaned the house and then began gardening, planting lettuce, onions, radishes, turnips, peas, and potatoes, then later oats, cucumbers, corn, tomatoes, watermelon, and muskmelon. Milford built frames and planted grapevines to train along them, and bordered the garden walks with decorative stones, so that the Spring Dell home became as lovely as it was useful.

Ellis was happier at the farm than she'd been in a long time. But this brief peace, like most in her life, was to be short-lived. For some time both she and Maggie had been studying nursing with Dr. Washington F. Anderson. He was a prominent man in Salt Lake and, although not a Mormon, had gained Brigham Young's respect and good will.

> Early in his residence in Salt Lake, he made it clear to Brigham that he did not claim to be a "convert" to the divine part of Mormonism, but that he admired the law and order that prevailed under Brigham's regime. It is said that Brigham Young slapped him on the shoulder, expressed the belief that he would become a convert in time, and assured him that he need have no fear of not enjoying full citizenship rights, including the privilege of medical practice. A strong sympathetic understanding developed between the two.[91]

It is not known if Dr. Anderson was ever baptized. But he assumed positions of leadership in the community and was elected president of the first Medical Society of Utah in the early 1870s. He had received his education at the University of Virginia and at the University of Maryland, Baltimore, and had a wide background of experience—political as well as medical, having been elected town magistrate and justice of the peace in Yolo, California. He was both skilled and dedicated, and he awakened many of Ellis's latent interests and ambitions. She found herself wanting to be *more* than a nurse. And there was much in the climate of the day to urge her on.

In 1867 Brigham had asked Heber John Richards to go east and study medicine. Heber, only twenty-seven years old, had just returned from serving a mission to England. But when Brigham said, "I want you to go to Bellevue Medical College to become a surgeon," Heber went.[92] Though it is interesting that the Church paid his expenses, as they had those of artists whom Brigham had sent to Paris to prepare themselves to work on murals for the Salt Lake Temple.

Only a year after the Mormons entered the Salt Lake Valley, while they were still housed in the walls of the old fort, Brigham had asked Dr. Willard Richards and his wife Hannah (who was an English nurse) to train some women in basic forms of care for the sick. And yet, during the year ending June 1850, "only one state or territory in the nation topped Utah's death rate of one person out of every forty-eight."[93]

This situation resulted somewhat from the primitive conditions the pioneers had lived in, and their lack of proper food and housing. It is also argued that the spiritual beliefs of the Mormon people discouraged medical practice among them.

Priesthood blessings, healings by faith, were very common — and though it is true that Brigham encouraged this in the people: "Don't run for a doctor until you have exercised the power of prayer. There is more healing in the laying on of hands than in all the physic you can pour down their throats"[94] — he also taught the practical side from the pulpit: "Spread lime. Be clean. Watch your children's diet. Keep their bowels open. Don't let them get the sore throat. . . ."[95] And by 1873, from valley to valley, he was crying enthusiastically, "The time has come for women to come forth as doctors in these valleys of the mountains."[96]

As always, what Brigham desired, what he envisioned had a way of becoming reality through his own power and the power of his people. Statistics gathered according to population indicated that during the last quarter of the nineteenth century the number of Utah women who studied medicine "could not be equaled in any other specific locality on the face of the earth."[97]

It was in the nature of women to be drawn to this both practical and compassionate field. "In most sections of the country, following an ancient pattern, women are striking back at the infirmities of the human race. As in earlier times, the one area of medicine that challenged the wit and strength of women was the practice of midwifery."[98] Hadn't Sister Eliza Snow herself stated that this medical training was vital "so that we can have our own practitioners, instead of having gentlemen practitioners. In ancient times we know that women officiated in this department, and why should it not be so now?"[99]

Journal entries by the men of the time contained merely a simple notation of a child's birth. In plural marriage families the name of the wife who became the mother would also be mentioned. "It is in the diaries of the women that we are swept up in the drama of certain obstetrical cases. And in the diaries of women who were not midwives we sense the struggle of mothers in childbirth. In the journals of some of the untrained, but Church-appointed midwives we see the courage of those women in coping with the problems of birth."[100]

Maggie and Ellis were in many ways sister-spirits as well as sister-wives, sharing common talents, goals, and feelings. They lived as their fellow women then lived, not questioning their motherhood, believing the principle that in the existence to come, all glory and progress would be based in the family unit, and children born in mortality would add to the glory of both woman and man. Plural marriage was practiced partly for this reason. Mormon women fulfilled their role as mothers as selflessly as they could, looking upon their children as their greatest blessing. Yet women's health, their very lives, were in constant danger. Ellis had mourned over this condition many times, had discussed the issue often, longing for the knowledge to save the lives of mothers and infants, longing for power to strike back at these unnecessary tragedies.

Although she and Maggie often talked over such problems, Ellis also discussed her feelings with Milford:

> Her husband was a tall man, affectionate and kind, and much loved by this beautiful dark-eyed wife. He himself was a person of intellect, but he was not the man to make a living for four wives. Ellis put the question fairly to Bard. Where the subject was dismissed by many a man with an angry word against his wife for wanting to go into the world as a female doctor, or as a breadwinner of any kind, he was not opposed to the idea. There was no stamp of the foot, no angry word. He was open-minded to the subject of medicine — willing that his wives should earn, glad for their cooperation, and so was the first to support Ellis in her ambitious plan.[101]

In 1872, just six years after Heber John Richards left for Bellevue, Romania Pratt stepped forward, the first woman to leave the territory to study medicine. Wife of Parley P. Pratt, Jr., and mother of six sons and one daughter, she sold the beloved piano she had inherited from her mother — which had been carefully carried across the plains — to finance her early studies in New York. She was forced to return after only one year to procure further funding. But her going had proven one thing: It could be done. She returned, not to New York, but to the Women's Medical College of Pennsylvania at Philadelphia. Founded in 1850 by Quakers, this was the first chartered, accredited female medical school in the

United States. It became the vanguard of all such institutions and has carried into our day a proud and outstanding reputation.

August and September of 1875 Ellis and her sister-wives spent in the city canning fruit. On October 4 Maggie left for medical school in Philadelphia. We have very few facts about the circumstances of her leaving or what led to her decision to actually go. She left a nine-month old baby behind in Mary's keeping. The first weeks were the hardest and there was no word from the busy ones at home. Ellis in her journal stated simply, "In four weeks she returned. Her loneliness and homesickness were so great she could not endure the separation."[102]

It had been a momentous step to take. Ellis had watched and loved and supported in silence. But Maggie had returned. What did that mean? Was this a dream that she and those like her had no right to dream?

Ellis had not been inactive during Maggie's absence. She had been taking quiet steps of her own. The persistent dream did not falter with Maggie's apparent failure, but teased at her mind and demanded attention despite her wavering will.

She had three major obstacles to face and overcome: Could she leave her children behind? Could she find sufficient funding? Could she conquer her own inadequacies and fears?

She discussed it time and again with Milford and he always assured her that she was capable, that she could rise to the challenge. She feared because of her lack of formal education. She had had almost no schooling except for her few months with Brother Maeser.

"My dear," Bard would reply, his eyes warm and patient, "*he* recognized your ability in the little work you did with him. Don't *I* know what you can do? Don't I know how you've always been up early, poring over your books before anyone else was stirring. Don't be afraid. I *know* you can succeed."[103]

There was one more opinion, one sanction she needed. She walked past the stone gate where the eagle hovered, wings spread gracefully, almost protectively, and through the door to the familiar rooms she loved so well. She found Brigham in his office. He received her with his usual kindness, and his eyes sparkled as he regarded her. Her own dark eyes shown with the earnestness of her purpose, as she stood in her graceful loveliness before him. He listened in his usual attentive manner; he asked questions; he nodded a time or two. He didn't offer official Church sanction, nor Church funding. But he granted her what she had come for, what she desired.

He stood, he walked over and took her hand — so small, so soft, so delicately boned — but capable, as capable as his own were. Hadn't he, Brigham, had sight of her greatness all along? "I say go, Ellis." His voice was warm and his keen gaze held hers. "Go, and God bless you."[104]

Surely with Brigham's benediction she could make it! Yet dozens of times, through the course of each passing day, as she gazed upon her young sons, as she heard their laughter, as she bent to kiss their foreheads and tuck them in bed, she wondered how she could possibly leave them. What in the world could be worth that kind of pain? What was wrong with her that she could even consider such madness?

But Mary had never had children of her own. She would love and nurture Ellis's; she had promised. Maggie was back, she would do her part in supporting Ellis. There was suddenly no reason left to postpone. She must either take the first awesome step forward, or forever turn her back on the longed-for dream.

5

New Challenges, New Horizons

On the morning of November 10, 1875, the Shipp family gathered, huddled and awkward, at the train depot. Ellis kissed each little boy's face, her eyes brimming. She picked up her baby, Burt, and held him to her. He was nearly fourteen months old; he could call her "mama," but he couldn't understand when she placed him in Mary's arms and quickly turned away from his outstretched hands.

Milford! She touched his face — so loved, so handsome. She clung to him, her heart trembling. Somehow she turned and walked the short distance that seemed like the space of forever between them. Then before she knew it the train was moving and they were waving. Their faces blurred as she tried to blink back the burning tears. They grew smaller and smaller until at last she turned from the window, no longer able to endure the painful sight.

> Moving swiftly along in the cars, I thought my heart would break this morning. Oh, for power, do I pray to endure this painful separation, and to gain the knowledge for which I have sacrificed so much. Never will I forget this morning — nor the sadness upon the faces of my loved ones as I bade them good-bye. The parting is too

painful to dwell upon. My heart aches so sadly I must endeavor to divert my thoughts, or I fear my strength will fail me.[1]

The journey was a singular experience for Ellis. The first lap she shared with sympathetic traveling companions — Elders Wood and Bullock and other missionaries who kindly helped her purchase her ticket in Omaha and see to the transfer of her belongings and baggage.

At first the scenery was dreary and barren, her nights tense and restless, affording her little rest. After crossing the Missouri she was forced to part from the missionaries, and the full weight of being "in a strange land, among strangers"[2] settled upon her. But she prayed for the spirit of the Lord to strengthen her and her prayers were answered.

On Friday, November 12, she found herself traveling through Iowa, her native state. "What strange sensations fill my heart," she recorded. " 'Twas here my parents dwelt, 'twas here that they loved and reared me for a number of years 'till the gospel's voice called them to a home in the distant west."[3]

On November 13 she crossed the Mississippi — by far the finest sight she had ever seen. But she didn't feel such enthusiasm for Chicago, that "terrible city"[4] where she was forced to wait a long hour and make her last difficult change of cars.

Sunday, the last day of her journey, was almost pleasant. The scenery along the Ohio River was truly lovely. And there was a fine old gentleman who engaged her in conversation. Their subjects inevitably led to religion. She bore her testimony to him with fervor and power. He was impressed with the beautiful, intense young woman who could speak so sincerely, so eloquently. His home was in Philadelphia, he told her, and he gave her his address and urged her to call upon him.

In the early hours of Monday morning, in the pre-dawn stillness, the train's shrill whistle shrieked the signal of their arrival in Philadelphia. People rubbed sleepy eyes and gathered their belongings, rushing out into the friendly warmth of the lighted station.

> A crowd, a rush, extending of welcoming hands, friendly greetings, loving embraces. Some hurrying one way, some that — and soon all were gone — and I was left alone.[5]

She had never felt so utterly lost and lonely. A policeman directed her to the waiting room. It seemed high and empty and filled with echoes and shadows. Then she noticed on one of the benches in the corner an old lady curled up asleep. What brought her to this place, Ellis wondered. Is she too a stranger here?

She chose a spot on one of the long benches, took her satchel, which had served for a pillow the last four nights, drew her shawl around her shoulders as some sort of cover, closed her tired eyes, and tried to sleep. But too many images played against her eyelids, too many questions fluttered across her mind. As soon as dawn streaked the sky, erasing the darkness, she made a hasty toilette and found a car to take her to 1324 Twenty-second Street. As she hoped, Sister Pratt was waiting there. Her kind greeting was like sun breaking through a gray mist. It was now full day, Monday morning, and there were things to be done.

At nine o'clock they went to the Women's Medical College to see Professor Bodley before the lecture began at ten. Ellis thought her "kind, refined, and dignified."[6] She paid her matriculation ticket of $5.00, professors ticket of $45.00, and gave her note for an additional $70.00. How strange she felt, how bewildered inside. But there was no time to doubt, no time to look backward. Her first class was about to begin. Head poised, eyes clear, she walked eagerly forward. This is what she wanted, this is what she had come for—she would not fail.

It didn't take long for her desires for knowledge to fully awaken. Ellis was struck by how much she did not know, but she loved the work—she loved the *learning*. If she had the association of the Saints and her family she could be perfectly happy in such a place. "But," she wrote, "perfect happiness is not designed in this life—we must not expect to have *all* of the desires of our hearts granted."[7]

Ellis took long walks, enthralled by the city, drawn to the elegant loveliness of the old homes. "How much I would appreciate having such a home," she confided to her journal, "a home where comfort and all the facilities for gaining knowledge and intelligence abound. This desire burns brightly tonight. 'Tis not alone for self, but for my darling children. Oh, I must succeed for their sakes—and my dear husband."[8]

She was amazed by how much hard work was required to gain a little knowledge. "If I only could retain what I hear!" she lamented.[9] She threw herself intensely into the work, so that it drew her up short when a lady told her, "You always appear so sad, my dear. As though you were grieving over something."[10] Did her countenance really impress others in such manner? She tried to be cheerful, or at least not melancholy. Did her aching heart really show so much on the surface?

Near the middle of January Sister Pratt requested that Ellis seek quarters elsewhere. Ellis's early rising interfered with her rest. Ellis cringed at the idea of going again among strangers, but knew such an arrangement would be for the best.

There were mornings she felt sad and lonely. She was bothered, too, with a pain in her side which sometimes was almost more than she could endure. "I sometimes have such burning desires for home that I feel like I could not live any longer away from my dear ones," she confessed.[11] But then she would receive a letter from home and be reminded of how eager Milford was for her to succeed. She must for his sake, if nothing else, have faith and be brave!

She found boarding with a Mrs. Wilson. She had to prepare her own food, which cut into her precious time. But she would make it up, she resolved, in organization and order.

Right before her birthday she received a letter from Grandfather Hawley, with a note from Grandmother and one from their little daughter, Sarah Ellis, born of the second wife who had died young, and cared for now by Grandmother as one of her own.

> My grandfather seems so happy in the great latter-day work. He seems to possess so much of the pure good spirit. How thankful I am after all these long years that he has accomplished all his work necessary for an exaltation in the kingdom of our Father. I pray that their lives may be preserved, that we may meet again. How dearly I love those truly kind parents.[12]

On January 20 she turned twenty-nine, just two years younger than her mother had been when she died. "But, Father," Ellis implored, "prolong my life, that I may live many years to do good in thy kingdom. Never did life seem to me so sweet and desirable."[13]

A new world was opening up to Ellis.

> Have just returned from the last lecture of the day. Dr. Hunt on the hystology of the nerves, truly interesting. The more I learn the more understandingly I can say "we are beautifully and wonderfully made."[14]

She often spent her holidays in the laboratory, though it might mean she would be doing her weekly wash till eleven, though it meant ignoring pain over her left thoracic cavity. Her days were long and the work demanding. At 7:00 P.M. on February 9 she recorded: "Since four this morning I have had no rest and must hurry up and eat my supper and go back to a demonstration of abdominal and pelvic cavities."[15]

Sometimes letters from home were a help, sometimes a hindrance.

> Received another letter, from my dear sister Mary. She says my sweet baby is such a comfort to her. I am so glad, poor girl. I feel so sorry that she has no children of her own. How rejoiced I should be if I could gain knowledge sufficient to restore her to a normal state that she might be blessed with offspring. — Received a letter from Maggie. A very good, kind letter, but notwithstanding its kindness and the presence of a twenty-dollar note, there were some things in it that I was weak enough to cry over. I have not shed many tears since I left home, for I have tried very hard to control my sensitive heart, but there are some things that cut to the depths, and it seems impossible to prevent the agonizing sensations.[16]

The best letters were, of course, from Milford. "Oh, how beautiful is life when we are beloved! With the love of my dear husband I can endure, can suffer anything and still be happy."[17]

Ellis loved the sensation of growth her learning gave her. She gained inner strength, although at times she was physically weak. One of the most difficult areas for her to handle and master was that of dissecting. An overwhelming sense of horror would overtake her. But she struggled against it, knowing she must subdue it. Eventually the light broke through to her spirit, and she was able to say, with the sound of joy:

> The horrifying dread that so oppressed me in the beginning is wearing off. All disagreeable sensations are lost in wonder and admiration. Most truly, "Man is the greatest work of God." Every

bone, muscle, tendon, vein, artery, and nerve seem to bear the impress of divine intelligence.[18]

This expanded spiritual vision was to color all she did in future years and add depth and power to her ministrations as a physician.

On February 22 Philadelphia celebrated George Washington's birthday. Ellis had never seen anything like it. After clinic at the Penn Hospital she and several companions made their way down densely crowded Chestnut Street to Independence Hall. She had never seen the liberty bell before, nor any of the relics she now gazed upon with such interest. She knew better than many of those pressing near her what freedom meant, how dear a price can be paid to gain it. With great tenderness she took in the new sensations.

Out on the street again she was amazed by the bustling and jamming, the vast number of people all crowded together. To walk down Chestnut Street was to "pass a succession of brilliant pictures."[19] The little shops boasting heavenly wares from Chinese silk and hand-painted porcelain to imported teas and exotic spices, looked especially grand with the stars and stripes waving from their windows. Her own spirits lifted with the wonderful sight.

March 3 was Milford's fortieth birthday. "I wonder how he feels tonight," Ellis mused. "May it be hopeful. Why should it not be so, with such brilliant attributes as he possesses?"[20] No matter how caught up she became with her studies and her demanding routine, her thoughts were never far from her loved ones. Sometimes the letters she received were so vividly written that she felt she was granted "a peep into that cherished sanctuary."[21] Lizzie was studying music on a serious level, hoping to achieve something of a professional nature. She had Ellis's wholehearted support. "I do hope Milford's wives may succeed in qualifying themselves for useful and profitable avocations in life," she wrote in her journal, "that we may not be such a weight and responsibility upon him, so that he will be able to follow pursuits best suited to his tastes and inclinations."[22]

March 16 was the commencement day for the medical class of 1876. It was bitter cold with rain and sleet. Twelve ladies received their M.D. degree. Ellis, watching, struggled with all her fears and inadequacies. She was not well; she had been working too many hard hours in the cold dissecting room. There had been no letter from home for weeks and she was worried. She listened to the address and watched the twelve happy women. Would she ever stand in their place, she wondered? The goal seemed so far away, so obscured. There were some lectures that had been given before her arrival and she was working ardently to make up lost material. Her weariness seemed to center in her eyes. Dr. Barton told her she must either stop using them so relentlessly or she must wear glasses. "The first I can't do," Ellis protested, "and the last I hope I will not be obliged to do."[23]

A typical day for Ellis began with a chemistry recitation at ten, lectures until one, dissecting till half past three, then a demonstration. In the evenings she returned for an anatomy recitation. On Monday, March 27, she rose at three, an hour earlier than she had intended, "but better too early than too late."[24] She carried out her usual morning program and spent the afternoon at practical anatomy, "tracing the delicate muscles of the face, that wondrous mechanical construction that gives the lights and shades of expression to the features. Truly in all things can we see the impression of divinity."[25]

In preparation for one of her anatomy recitations she was charged to find out why the soles of the feet and the insides of the hands of the Negro are not black like the other surfaces of his body. When class was held Dr. White asked for Ellis's explanation. She answered that she thought the pigment was not there.

"How is that?" the professor queried. Ellis replied, "I believe it to be a design of the great Creator, which like many of His other works, is alike wonderful and incomprehensible."[26]

It took courage for her to reply in this manner. Dr. White was a believer in Huxley and Darwin, and Ellis knew that. But she was able to see herself in a healthy, realistic light. She confided in her journal that Dr. White doubtlessly smiled at her "credulity." "But I thank heaven for the faith that illumines my soul," she recorded. "What would this life be without it!"[27]

In early spring there was some excitement at the college con-

cerning a resolution to charge the students an additional fee of
$2.50 for use of the pharmaceutical laboratory. There was much
protesting among the students until Dr. Pierce gave them some
firm, practical advice and explained the matter. The college received its support from gentlemen who gave freely because of their
interest and dedication, who received no interest whatever on their
money. He softened their anger and reminded the students of their
privilege which others were helping to provide.

The college had gone from the stage of encountering violent
opposition to an intermediate stage of partial consent, and finally
came into the light of acceptance. Its pioneers had lived to see their
dreams come true. Just the year before Ellis arrived the cornerstone
had been laid on the new building, "in the name of Woman and
for Her Advancement in the Science and Practice of Medicine."[28]

The college, located on the corner of North College Avenue
and Twenty-first Street, was "a handsome four-story brick building
with a frontage of nearly two hundred feet."[29] It was arranged with
all the lecture rooms on one floor, easy stairs, ample cloakroom
and toilet arrangements and carefully screened windows; in other
words, singularly adapted to women, or so the designers felt.
Its order of lectures and examinations closely paralleled those of
the University of Pennsylvania. When Ellis attended there was no
entrance examination, but three graded winter sessions were required for graduation. At the completion of the first session there
would be preliminary exams in chemistry, anatomy, and physiology. Weekly quizzes were part of the regular instruction, with an
abundance of laboratory work.

In the spring when the weather improved, Ellis indulged in
several outings. She possessed an inherent love of nature, and
springtime always brought these deep feelings to life. But now she
was experiencing something new: a large, crowded city, the over-
abundance of buildings and people. Ellis could often be close to
eloquent in her expression. One beautiful Sabbath morning in
April she expressed the following:

> The marts are closed, the haunts of men are deserted and for so
> large and vast a city the quiet, the reigning stillness is supreme and
> sublime, and each soul "follows the dictates of his own conscience"

and worships in that manner which may best please him. On every hand are towering spires of lofty temples, built that men might worship God therein.[30]

The many varied religions amazed her mind. Her own strong religious convictions rose to the surface and she longed to be able to share them, to bless others' lives, to see "all worship in the same manner and bow together unitedly at the same altar."[31]

That same Sabbath evening, at Sister Pratt's insistence, she went to a religious meeting at Lincoln Hall, but was repulsed by what she heard and saw there. A week later she attended a meeting of the Friends. "What a strange manner to worship the Lord," she responded. "Who would not be a Saint?"[32]

In May she attended a Baptist church. The reverend, Mr. Henson, was an eloquent speaker. As they walked home together Romania Pratt asked her, "Can Brother Shipp speak that well?"

Ellis, encouraged, expressed her profuse and loving opinion, then apologized for her "seeming egotism."

"You are indeed excusable," Romania replied with a smile. "It is a pleasure to me, for it is so seldom I see a woman who has such an exalted opinion of her husband as you possess."[33]

Ellis's work by now was progressing beautifully.

> Began the study of blood, chemically. How interesting and delightful are my studies. I used to think the study of medicine so dry and obtruse, and how erroneous were my impressions! I think that it causes everything in nature to be fraught with greater interest. How happy must be a thoroughly educated person, for even the cursory knowledge I have gained in the last few months has opened to my view depths and heights of which I had never dreamed.[34]

Her magnificent spirit and mind were coming into their own; she had found a new source of joy in existence.

Ellis was thrilled by a compliment she received in her chemistry class. Professor Bodley, after applying the test for hydrocyanic acid, turned to the class and said, "Now we will have the equations. Who has finished?" She turned to Ellis. "Mrs. Shipp, let us have yours."

Ellis trembled. She was afraid she had done something wrong. "Before I had scarcely uttered the last symbol she exclaimed, 'Why,

that is right and well done and indeed shows very marked advancement.' She gave *me* the honor. *I* gave it to my Heavenly Father."[35]

Ellis was particularly fascinated with the study of obstetrics.
"This is to me the most interesting part of my studies. To
understand this and the diseases of children shall be my greatest
object for the next two years. I think there could be no greater
accomplishment in the medical line than to be able to treat these
conditions and diseases successfully."[36]

Though personal preference strongly inclined her to this one
field, Ellis had a clear grasp of the overriding goal, the total picture.

> How wonderful to a reflecting mind is the intimate relation-
> ship existing between all sciences. As we trace the different branches
> we find them all linking with each other in one grand chain of il-
> limitable knowledge, the lengths and depths of which the mortal
> mind cannot fathom.[37]

In addition to the regular sessions of the college, there was a
spring term which was strongly recommended. Ellis went through
all sorts of agonies deciding whether she ought to stay, whether she
would be able to stay, how she would manage financially. She had
contemplated going home for a visit. But it was arranged instead
that she stay and study and Milford would pay her a visit there.

"I feel thankful that I don't have to leave here this summer,"
she confided. "I think if I can but master the *theory* of medicine, the
practice will not be so difficult a matter for me, and I will confine
myself to my textbooks this summer."[38]

Knowledge and training were amply available to every student who chose Philadelphia as a working ground; almost un-
believably so.

> Within the limits of the city are thirteen general hospitals and
> fourteen for the treatment of special classes of diseases and injuries.
> In addition to these are four hospitals for lying-in and the diseases of
> women, and two for the diseases of children, with eight general and
> six special dispensaries.[39]

On Friday, May 12, Ellis received a "soul-thrilling tribute"
from Milford, written on their wedding anniversary. Her response
shows her rare understanding of the nature of men:

> Few women receive such testimonials of their husband's
> affection. Man is not naturally as demonstrative as woman, but

when their emotional natures do hold sway, what depth of feeling do they portray.[40]

Her love for Milford was the most spiritual, all-consuming thing in her existence.

> 'Tis sweet to love, I think indeed it is to those who love most, who are most Godlike. Not the base and groveling passion that the world calls love, but love pure and chaste, based upon the intrinsic attributes of the soul. This is the kind of love that satisfies my nature, and may I ever be worthy of it.[41]

On May 18 Romania Pratt left for Boston. Ellis accompanied her to the depot and said goodbye. "Friend after friend depart," she murmured.[42] She returned home with despondent spirits. In the gathering twilight her little room seemed lonely and dark. She had neglected to obtain matches, and was too weary now to go get them. She climbed into bed and the quiet gloom settled round her. It was long, too long, before sleep came "to quell the troubled tide of thought" that swept across her soul.[43]

May drew to a close and so did the long months of loneliness and dedication. Ellis was at work in the pharmaceutical laboratory when letters from home were brought. One bore Milford's name; she opened it first and most eagerly. He was coming! He was actually on his way! She rejoiced in her usual irrepressible manner: "It is said that sudden and extreme joy sometimes consumes life. Be that as it may, I thought for a moment I should surely faint."[44]

And there was another cause for joy, good news to tell him. Ellis had been given the mistaken idea, the cruel false hope that she might complete her education in less than the required full three winter terms by using spring terms as partial compensation and thus requiring her to be absent from her loved ones just two and one half calendar years. When she discovered that she would be required to spend a complete three years in attendance, the knowledge was nearly more than she could bear.

Professor Bodley kindly suggested that she write to the faculty explaining her individual predicament, which she did, outlining what she would do to compensate for the lost six months, explaining how far from home she was, what difficulties she would encounter with scheduling and financing. She had just received a reply—in unanimous favor of her petition. This was contrary to the college's laws, but for her the faculty made an exception, having learned what hard work she was performing and believing that she understood herself and what she was doing here.

On June 2 Ellis boarded the car for Thirty-second and Market Depot and waited for the 2:30 train to pull in. Soon she heard the shrill report of the whistle, the hiss and screech of the huge steam-driven wheels. Now there were people pouring out of the doors onto the landing. In a moment she recognized the familiar face, tan and lean and wonderfully handsome. She ran to meet him.

Ellis was about to begin upon one of the most delightful times of her life. She had never known any honeymoon with Milford. Even though their early married days were happy and tranquil, they were still interspersed with the ordinary responsibilities of day-to-day life. And for so long now she had had only a share of Milford; part rather than the whole she intensely desired. Here they were alone with no interference, no jealousies, no other demands.

They went sightseeing all over Philadelphia, and she shared with him the places she'd come to love. The Centennial Exposition was then in progress. She and Bard crossed the long bridge that led to the Lansdowns entrance, explored the marvels of the Electrical Building, glided up the Schuylkill on a double-decked, blunt-nosed paddle boat, watched the elegant visitors strolling—women with gay parasols and ribbon-bedecked bonnets, men with soft-hued Homburg hats. There were moments when they no longer saw what went on about them, when Ellis begged Bard to re-create what she'd missed for her: Which son fetched the coal, which cut the kindling? Who milked the cow? Did little Richie really carry the full bucket across the street for five cents a quart? What did Mary say of her baby? Could he run yet? How many words did he speak? Did she sing him a lullaby at bedtime? The questions would fly while her brown eyes glowed.

One day they went sailing on the Delaware River, boarding a boat named "Perry" at a crowded wharf. She had never seen a ship in full sail, nor the fascinating steamboats and smaller vessels. They passed the military academy and Fort Delaware, turned up Salem Creek, and disembarked at the city. They spent hours strolling the narrow, quaint streets there, admiring the old wisteria-covered homes, gathering flowers, leaves, even moss and lichens. She had never been this carefree since she was a girl. Not a ripple marred the day's pleasure. They stood in awe before a majestic old oak, well over one hundred years old, with thirty-two trunks, each one as large in girth as a regular tree. This kind of quiet permanence didn't exist in the settlements of Utah. In the early evening they returned to Ingersol Street and Ellis tucked the treasured day in her memory's store to be one of the few perfect pieces she kept there.

At Milford's insistence, nearly two weeks after his arrival, she called upon Dr. Cleaveland concerning her health. The doctor wasn't satisfied with her diagnosis so he made an appointment at the Woman's Hospital the following morning so that Dr. Broomall, who was extremely adept in diagnosing heart problems, might have a look at Ellis as well.

Ellis didn't want to keep the appointment. The doctors told her what she most feared to hear. They advised her to return home and take a respite from her studies, take the medicine they prescribed for her, and do all she could to restore her health.

"You must not try to be a doctor," one of them told her. "Your heart is skipping beats. You might not live, my dear, more than six months."

"So many of my sisters are dying when they have their babies," Ellis responded. Her dark eyes were moist, but her voice was firm. "Someone must be trained to try to save them."[45]

But she knew there was wisdom in their advice to take care of herself now. That didn't mean she couldn't come back and go on. Bard, while he whispered, "Ellis, come home with me, Ellis," also promised she could return in the fall. She gazed into his kind brown eyes and believed the promise.

She packed her trunks, her feelings too tangled to sort through. "I had hoped to return a graduate," she lamented, "but oh, how far I feel from it now. I can see but one joy before me—my *children*, my precious children!"[46]

On June 19 she left Philadelphia, boarding the cars that would take her westward and home. She felt stunned, and a sense of gloom seemed to cloud her. "Had I but accomplished all that I came for, how joyfully would I turn my face homeward. But I feel dissatisfied; my work is unfinished. Oh, how will all this end? I pray my Father to overrule all for the best, but how dark is the outlook now."[47]

Milford was overjoyed to have his wife once again. He had not anticipated the void she would leave behind her. He was a busy man; he was somewhat introspective; he had three other women to see to his wants and needs. How then, could this lovely, delicate creature before him — eyes burning with warmth and sparkling with light — fill his thoughts and cause such emotions within him? All she had meant to him when they were young was now rekindled. He wanted to see the smile light her face, hear her sweet girlish voice — he wanted her with him!

Ellis, too, was drawn to the joy of what lay before her. "Milford as my traveling companion, the dream of my life realized at last!"[48]

At four in the afternoon they arrived in Washington and took rooms at the Miliden Hotel. Ellis thought it the finest city she had ever seen, with such beauty and architectural variety. They visited with George Q. Cannon and his wife and she felt how wonderful it was to be in the society of Saints once more.

Tuesday morning they strolled through the famous streets, up Pennsylvania Avenue to the Capitol. Ellis was deeply aware of the significance of what they were doing.

> The walks that have been trodden by the great men of the land since the days of the illustrious Washington are still the same, and the stone steps are even wearing away by the constant tramping of feet that profess to be marching on for the weak of the nation. How long a person may live and still know nothing of life.[49]

At ten in the morning, on board the vessel "Arrow," they sailed down the Potomac to Mount Vernon. Ellis was awed by the expansive Navy Yard and Fort Washington with its gaping portholes "staring defiance to all intruders."[50] The green grass that bordered the banks of the river, the drooping willows that trailed at the water's edge, seemed sadly at odds with the large guns and stacked ammunition, which spoke too realistically of cruelty and war.

After leaving Washington, Ellis suffered a bout of motion

sickness, becoming too weak to even hold up her head. She was more grateful than ever for Milford's presence, for his tender, understanding care. "As I watched his beloved features," she recorded, "I think he never looked so handsome before."[51]

Ellis had a poetic nature and a flowing, poetic way of expressing herself. As the train rolled through the green prairies of Illinois and Iowa she was struck by the profusion of beauty around her: the lush grass and trees in so many shades of green, the sweet wild roses, the violets and lilies. They stirred memories of her childhood, but even more clearly drew mind-pictures of the little faces she'd left behind, her darling boys whose delight it was to pick flowers for Mama.

"As I am swept swiftly on by the wonderful power of steam," she mused, "powerless to stretch forth my hand and pluck these beauteous flowers, I am reminded of life. In the busy onward march we rush thus madly on in pursuit of worldly gain in our onward struggle, too busy to gather the flowers along the wayside. Oh, if it were only for pleasure, Mama would never more leave you sweet flowers for aught else that life could give — but for your future good I must sacrifice my own joys."[52]

Only those closest to her realized that the moving impulse behind her self-discipline, her great deeds, was to brighten and improve the lives of her husband and children. This impulse, this almost pure incentive, would sustain her and them for the rest of her life.

The train stopped at Council Bluffs and again touched old feelings and memories. How many countless Saints had suffered here? "There is but One," Ellis recorded, "who fully knows those sufferings."[53]

Now the train, so swift before, seemed to move in slow motion. She became feverish to reach home! "Over the plains, the dreary, monotonous plains . . . only one more night and then, oh then — "[54]

On June 28 the train reached Salt Lake City. "The happiest moments I ever experienced were this night when I clasped my darlings in my arms."[55] She was home. Right now nothing else could matter but to hold and love her little ones again.

6

The Pain and the Prize

Being home was like a gift to Ellis. For many days she savored it as one would a soft breeze on the skin, a sweet taste on the tongue. Then as the realities set in she became slowly frightened. She could see that Bard's promise would not be easy to keep. There were so many unforeseen influences that seemed waiting to prevent it.

There was jealousy on the part of the others. Why should Ellis be the only one to have dreams come true? Though unspoken, the pressures were there — the subtle resentment, the quiet opposition. Besides, it would be a burden on everyone if she chose to return. The bleakness of her financial situation was no longer softened. Previously she had been far away, removed. Now the facts stared back at her cold, unrelenting.

These were mountains to overcome, but one more had been added, one more that made her fond dreams melt away as wet dew when the full morning sun burns off its brightness. She had discovered that she was pregnant. Certainly, nothing could be attempted now!

The fact struck her with the full force of its consequent brooding, its consequent tearing apart of all the dreams which, in the last year she had built for herself. She moped until her spirit was almost torn asunder by the clash between the threat to her profession and the love of her unborn child. She became morbidly attached to the other children, thinking she could never tear herself away from them again. Maddened by her self-indulgence which she recognized, fully aware of her sentimentality, she fell into a kind of despondency and doubt that she could not set aside.[1]

No one was any help to Ellis now. Not Mary, who sometimes had power to soothe her. Not Bard who, in spite of his gentleness, had no answers, no means with which to change the unchangeable.

There was only one source of strength she could turn to. With His help she could pull herself out of the darkness. Hadn't she done so many times before? She turned to that God who had always known her, with whom she had shared the depths of despair and pain, with whom she had communed on the sunniest heights of rejoicing.

In 1872 the Patriarch John Smith had given Ellis a blessing. Now, in her extremity, she turned to his words:

> Sister Ellis, listen to the promptings of the Spirit and thy guardian angel shall whisper in thy ear and give thee counsel in time of need and strength in time of trial. Thy name shall be borne in honorable mention from generation to generation. Let thy heart be comforted, for better days await thee. Thy table shall be blessed with the bounties of the earth. Then shalt thou clothe the naked and feed the hungry. Thou shalt have the gift of healing and be crowned with the mothers of Israel.[2]

Gradually the determination that was part of her glorious nature grew and strengthened and rose to assist her. She would just have time to complete the school term before the birth of her baby. With that quiet resolution now apparent, she told Bard that she would return to Philadelphia; she would not abandon her goal.

He and the other members of the household were astonished. But Ellis neither argued nor explained. Time was short and she would have much preparation. She refused to allow herself to wonder and worry as to how it would all work out. She spent her energies doing all she could from day to day.

During this time Ellis gave a series of weekly lectures Saturday mornings at eleven in the office of the *Woman's Exponent,* following a session by Dr. Seymour Young. These hour-long lessons were studiously prepared and well received. The *Exponent* printed a synopsis of her material and listed the main points she considered vital for success:

> First, a natural love for the profession; Second, a strong will and firm determination of purpose "that no common obstacle can hinder"; Third, strong nerves and power to control one's emotional nature; Fourth, good health; Fifth, suitable textbooks; Sixth, competent teachers; Seventh, clinical advantages; and Eighth, undisturbed time.[3]

Ellis placed love for the profession at the head of the list and reminded her listeners "that to benefit and bless our fellow creatures is the greatest and grandest aim of mortals; that in God's kingdom there should be no thought of self-aggrandizement, but the welfare of His people."[4]

Ellis knew whereof she spoke and her power shone through as she gazed with glowing eyes at her listeners and said, "With a resolute will and faith in God none can surpass the women of Utah whom the world pities so supremely."[5]

One evening, while reading the newspaper, Ellis saw a notice that made her heart skip a beat. A group of Saints, heading east for schooling and missions, was leaving on a special train the following morning. She read the notice to Milford. He didn't reply. Ellis held her breath through the waiting silence.

"Do you really want to be on that train?" His voice, whisper-soft, held a note of pleading that made her tremble.

"Yes, oh yes," she replied. Could he understand? He *must* understand — must remember his promise, remember the sacrifice that had already been spent.

He knew her. He knew he could not stop her; he dared not deter her from what she considered a holy course. With his consent she began making preparations.

It would take all night to complete her packing. Feverishly she worked through the still, dark hours. Never had she prayed as she did that night. One of her boys was suddenly ill with a sore throat and high fever. Could this be an omen of heaven to keep her home? Was she foolish, selfish, wicked to think to leave him? Was she turning her back on her rightful place? Why did she feel so right about it—so driven, so destined to go this way?

As dawn broke over the far mountains, softening the peaks, flooding into the valley, she went to her son's room. He opened his eyes and smiled when he saw her.

"Mama, I'm not sick anymore. I'm almost well."

Surely this was the answer she had been seeking! The tears filled her eyes as she held him to her. After a few moments she left and went to her own room. Perhaps she might lie down for a few moments' rest. Bard found her there and approached her gently.

"Ellis, I wonder if it's right for you to go."

She jumped out of bed, awake and trembling. "Don't talk like that!" It was half indignation, half plea. "Yesterday you said it was all right. Neither of us must falter now."[6]

She would allow no objections to undermine her decision, no feelings to penetrate and crumble its foundation.

> But as the train rolled away, and looking from the rear platform, she saw three of her boys standing barefoot on the frosty ground of the early September morning, she herself wondered if she was right. The question haunted her until she could find no peace. If she could succeed, if she could succeed—the words matched the rhythm of the train—her boys could have shoes. They could wear them in summer as well as winter if they wanted to. If she succeeded thousands of babies would live to wear shoes in the summer.[7]

The train had a layover of several hours in Ogden, so Ellis visited Brother and Sister Franklin, spent several pleasant hours in their home, and picked up some dress models Maggie had left there almost a year before. She had hopes they would help see her through her college expenses. "I am so anxious not to be any expense to Milford," she recorded, "and I pray my Father to prosper me and open the way for the selling of these models."[8]

She spent September 29 on the train, the third anniversary of the date of Anna's death. It threw her into one of her deep, contemplative moods. She felt she was assuming a task which she had not strength to accomplish, but she held no illusions concerning her inner motives: it was for the future advantage of her children that she suffered, that she deprived herself of the joy of their present association.

The thing that worried her the most deeply right now was Milford. This was the very first time in their married life she had gone against him; the first time their impressions had been so diametrically opposed. She had not left with Milford's blessing. "I know he wishes me well and feels kindly toward me, but oh, his impressions, how dare I go contrary to them?"[9]

She was becoming her own person and it was a painful process, an alien sort of thing for a plural wife of the 1870s to do. She had accepted Milford's direction, Milford's decisions in all things as final. Now she was casting all else aside and following her own inner lights.

There was a young man on the train with whom Ellis held several interesting conversations. She described him as "educated and intellectual."[10] She was keenly aware of the advantages of learning and refinement, and wished that her children might have them in her own home. She had a testimony that the perfect condition would be a home that combined the truths of the gospel with "the sunlight of intellectuality."[11]

The journey was long and extremely trying. She arrived in Omaha late at night and was forced to put up at the Emigrant House till the following morning. She rose at three o'clock, ate a miserable breakfast, and went to the depot to obtain her ticket but no one was there. She waited nearly an hour for the clerk to arrive, but by then the train was preparing to move out. By the time she had her ticket and her baggage in order the train had already begun to move! She ran alongside calling for help, but no one heard her. So she tossed her bundles in and climbed on behind them, sitting right where she was until someone came along to assist her.

At last she arrived at her destination, weary and with a future looming before her that only the most courageous would have dared to brave.

Milford had given her all the money in his possession, barely more than enough for her fare and her fees. She hoarded carefully the little store that was left her, subsisting on a diet of bread and milk, spending fifty cents a week at the grocers. She did make arrangements to trade breadstuff with the baker in exchange for teaching his daughter how to sew. She had approached him with her cherished models, which were nothing more than simple pieces of cardboard cut to the size and shape of the human figure. A skilled seamstress could design any fashion from them. Ellis, when only a child, had developed such skill. All these years later, in such strange, dark circumstances her mother's patient training came back to light and bless her.

Ellis stayed late each day in the dissecting room or library until the janitor would come to lock the doors. This saved on heat and light in her own room. Her only recreation was writing letters home, and she lived on the letters her family sent her, gaining more sustenance from them than she did from the bread and the occasional piece of bacon she allowed herself.

When the doctors discovered her condition they were shocked and warned darkly that it would be impossible for her to continue. The strain of dissecting, attending operations, performing all the strenuous tasks that would be required for graduation, would most assuredly harm both her and her child. They pleaded with her to consent to a forced labor.

Ellis endured her Gethsemane. She prayed all through the night for strength and guidance, on her knees in her little attic room. As dawn broke through the window her answer broke through the veil of darkness. She knew what she had to do. She could answer them now, "I came to learn how to save life, not to take it!"[12]

Her answer rang through the air when she ceased speaking. It rings still, with a power that thrills us. These women of the world, cultured and learned, knew little of the strengths of this woman from Utah, "her determination, her depth of purpose, her all-encompassing love, her abiding faith in her Heavenly Father."[13] She disguised her figure with a black dolman and attended classes, not missing a single session through all the school year.

On November 10 she reached the one-year mark. Only eighteen months more to go. Surely one day at a time she could make it.

But by Christmas she was beginning to wonder. She was alone in her chill and dismal quarters, but happy with the thought that the loved ones at home were well. Milford's letters for months had been anxious and troubled; he had been unable to make any money since Ellis left. Bravely she kept her own struggles private, never adding one bit to his already heavy load. Just before Christmas a letter arrived that cheered her. He had succeeded in selling enough canned fruit to stock a generous supply of provisions to last through the winter.

Still, the holidays seemed to drag. Philadelphia was bursting with shoppers, the old streets bright and festive. She had only memories and imagination's eye to draw her a picture of what Christmas Day at home with her children might be like. She had no means to make her own day cheerful, or mark it in any special way. When New Year's morning came she had only one dollar. She had never dreamed that a new year would find her in such straits: pregnant, alone, with no money and little prospect of obtaining some. She would have to miss vital lectures she ought to be attending and go out and try to sell models door to door.

At times she wondered if perhaps she was being punished for her "blindness and obstinacy."[14] But the doubts she felt were only fleeting. She kept her faith in her Heavenly Father. "I believed He would let nothing come upon me but what would be for my good, even though it should be want and suffering, and I resolved to bear patiently whatever might come."[15]

While she sat pondering her circumstances she heard the postman's ring, then more wonderfully, her own name called. There would be news from home! She took her letter, and was surprised when she opened it to discover that the contents came from her sister-wife Lizzie, who had been gone from home for some time visiting her own mother. There was something else inside the letter. Her heart pounding, Ellis drew it out. It was a money order for fifty dollars, all earned by Lizzie's own patient labor, and all for Ellis.

It was impossible to hold back the grateful tears. She knew that her Heavenly Father was mindful of her, that he wouldn't let her suffer more than she could bear. She also felt renewed strength to face tomorrow. So many were sacrificing to keep her here. For their sakes, to fulfill their faith, to return their favors she must— she would—continue and succeed.

Ellis's thirtieth birthday came but she scarcely noticed, so immersed was she in her studies and her work. She seemed to have thrown off any remnant of self-pity or depression and displayed a spirit bright with joy and hope. However, she was still young enough to look upon thirty as being old.

> How strange it seems that I am so old. Still I do not *feel* old. It seems to me my morning of life has just dawned, there is so much in life to live for, so much to accomplish. Hope beams brightly — and energy is strong and by the aid of my Heavenly Father I hope to make my life one of usefulness upon the earth. [16]

Thinking, learning, growing brought Ellis great joy, and she felt the increase in her strength and wisdom. In March on Bard's birthday she recorded one of the beautiful insights that were part of her nature, which were coming now more and more frequently.

> Throughout this day has all my energy been involved in scientific investigations, for soon will come the day of "final examination" and every moment must be utilized in reviewing my studies. But thanks to Him who constructed the wondrous mechanism of the human soul, even in the most severe mental strain there are still other filaments which can extend and link themselves with *heart thoughts*, though time be not ours to give them utterance. While the "mind's eye" has followed the intricacies of study, the *eye of love* has beheld in vivid imagination its ideal, its Bard upon the bright anniversary day, that completes the cycle of another year. Methinks the years of our life are our greatest wealth, for only in time can we gain experience and only through experience, the most perfect knowledge. [17]

The winter term came to an end and Ellis had distinguished herself, passing anatomy, physiology and chemistry with high marks and winning the esteem of her professors for her performance and perseverance. She attributed her success to that higher power that was always there to help her and see her through. She could see now the possibility of success, of completion of what had before been a dream.

> Heaven knows it is not for *self* I have thus absented myself from all that earth holds so dear. 'Tis not for worldly praise I labor early and late, but that I may become a more competent wife and mother and better qualified for all the duties of *woman*, and of a Saint of God. [18]

When Milford learned of her high scores he wrote congratulating Ellis.

I had no idea (knowing your opportunities, etc.) that you would be so successful in your examinations. I think it most remarkable, for I regard your examinations this spring a greater difficulty to encounter than they will be next spring. I think your standing is worthy of all praise, and should satisfy the most ambitious. Allow us to congratulate you most earnestly on your triumph, for triumph under the circumstances it is most assuredly.[19]

Halfway into the spring term Ellis chose the theme for her thesis: "The Function of Generation," an ambitious subject for her to undertake, but one that excited her most keen interest.

In April Lizzie gave birth to a little girl and was blessed through some difficulties by the power of faith. In relating the details to Ellis, Milford added:

So let us encourage you, and say to you, the Lord will bless you and preserve you from all evil and in your approaching confinement you will be blessed far above any blessing you ever received before, and your heart will rejoice in His great goodness to you in your hour of sickness. So be of good cheer, for all will be well with you. Have no fear, for no evil will come unto you.[20]

At last, the blessing her heart had prayed for! She felt that her husband's words were given through the power and inspiration of the Holy Spirit, and though she knew not where she would go or what she would do at the time of the birth, her heart was comforted, and she felt indeed that all would be well with her.

May brought her eleventh wedding anniversary and thoughts of the man she loved and had left behind. She wrote him a long, nostalgic letter recalling the joy of their wedding day, reaffirming her faith in the interweaving of their spirits, the strengthening of their love through the years of change.

Ellis was racing against the clock now, finishing vital classwork, hoping the baby would wait till her work was complete. Dean Bodley, the gentle Quaker lady, with wavy white hair and fine, kind eyes, had always stood at the head of the school as a friend and adviser, as someone the students loved, someone strong enough to approach with their problems. Ellis went to her to request a room in the charity ward when the time of her child's birth arrived.

Dean Bodley arched her eyebrows and pursed her small mouth as she listened. She admired this lovely Mormon girl. She, of course, was tolerant of all religions. But Mormonism? If the stories were true, the awful tales one heard hissed and whispered, then they certainly couldn't prove it by what she had known! John W. Young, a brother of Brigham's, had been an acquaintance of hers years ago in New York. He was an extraordinary man, one she respected. And now there was this courageous, intelligent girl . . . She took Ellis's cool, slender hand in her own small plump one and assured her that only the best of care would be offered her at the time of confinement. She arranged for a private hospital room, and for living arrangements at Dr. Young's home, where she would be cared for until the baby's arrival.

Ellis was impressed by the beauty and peace of her new surroundings, grateful for the sincere kindness extended her there. On May 25 at nine minutes to seven in the morning, Dr. Young, who officiated at the birth, laid a beautiful, perfect baby girl in her mother's arms. Sister Pratt was there, adding love and support. Ellis reached out hungrily for the infant. A child, any child, was a miracle. But a daughter—she had been blessed with another girl! She had felt so alone; she had longed for Milford. But now this precious gift was here. The women looking on shared Ellis's wonder. Nothing like this had ever happened at the college before. Mother and child were looked upon by all present "as one of the seven wonders of the world."[21]

For three luxurious weeks Ellis and the baby basked in attention and fond care. The baby grew and Ellis gained strength and mended . . . and dreamed. A year ago at this time she had sailed with Milford down the Delaware River to Salem—that honeymoon day that had been bright with perfect love and pleasure. Now, though she could not be near Milford or her children, she had her little Olea to love. Not once did she seem concerned or resentful, wondering how she would care for a baby during the months to come. She took one day at a time and was caught up in pleasure, pleasure and Ellis-type gratitude.

Near the end of June the respite ended. She moved back to Mrs. Wilson's boarding house, taking a room on the third floor at five dollars a month.

> But with what reluctance do I leave this haven of rest. How much more desirable is life when one can be surrounded with even a moderate degree of life's comforts and luxuries; especially when one can be in constant communication with the refined and the intellectual. As steel sharpeneth steel so does the contact of mind with mind.[22]

These were the things Ellis wanted for her children, the refining influences and opportunities for which she labored.

> I must not murmur—I must be diligent and renew my studies —my sweet babe must have every care and attention requisite for her health, besides my other numerous duties. So I have in reality no time for idle repining.[23]

Indeed, her work was cut out for her. She hired a competent woman, Emma Buch, to come in mornings and care for Olea. She was up late washing, up early ironing. Up early again going through the wards, obtaining vital experience in diagnosing. Spare time she spent completing her thesis.

Summer came; the humid, oppressive New England summer. The night of July 3 Ellis lay awake, her ears ringing "with the snapping, cracking, banging and roaring of artillery."[24] All the next day the noise continued, bright flags waved from nearly every window, the streets shook with the laughter of hundreds of children celebrating the glorious day. One note gives us insight into Ellis's feelings: "How are my little ones this day?"[25] It was painful watching the childish faces when she was denied even one glimpse of the ones she loved.

Ellis was not able to obtain admission into the hospital for the summer session and this was a great disappointment to her. She had a testimony of the importance of practical experience and was learning so much from the obstetric cases, cancer cases, and others she was working on. By August she had made the decision to take her baby and go off to the country for a while. She would try to sell models; the change would be much better than the breathless, stagnant heat of the city. But one of the hospital cases she was involved in dragged on and she couldn't break away yet. On August 28 she received a letter from Milford with the sad news that Mary had lost her little boy—her only child. For so many years Mary had prayed and longed for children. Now death robbed her of all her treasure, her heart's whole store.

The following day, August 29, Ellis started bright and early with Olea for Arch Street Wharf where they boarded the steamer *Perry* for Salem. The baby was delighted with the crowd, the sounds, and the music. But Ellis could not stop thinking of her sister, Mary, of the terrible loss she had just endured. She, herself, had lost children, true, but she had others. She had lost her first darling daughter, Anna, but was blessed with another one now, perfect and sweet. Mary's sufferings blunted the edge of her own pleasure and deepened her sense of gratitude.

Ellis was, above all else, a true mother, intelligently dedicated to this role in life. She wrote at this time in her journal:

> Often I hear women murmuring at the fate that gives them children. But oh, it is to me the crowning joy of a woman's life to be a mother, and to feel that love welling from the heart that is a joy to the giver and the receiver. What nobler mission in life than to be a *faithful mother*. Joyful will be the day when I can gather my little flock into their fold and perform for them the duties of a mother.[26]

The "duties of a mother" as Ellis saw them were widely extended and varied and she performed them brilliantly and well through a long life of sensitivity and service to her "heart's best treasures."

The ride to Salem was a trip back in time for Ellis. This same boat had carried her and Milford just a little over a year ago. But then each sight, each sensation had thrilled her. Now, without Milford near her, where was the joy? Life was so much brighter when there was a loved one to share it with you.

They landed in Salem in the early afternoon. The intense heat dragged at Ellis, but she rallied her spirits, gathered her bags and her baby and hurried to the nearest house to inquire where there might be rooms to let. The kind old lady who answered the door could not help her, but she offered her a glass of cool milk and the services of her little granddaughter to accompany her and carry her parcels.

Together they tried several places, but each was filled. At last someone directed them to "'Shafer's Hotel." Ellis was weary with the sun and the weight of the baby and was grateful to accept a night's lodging there, even if it was only temporary. She ate her first good meal of the day and retired to bed, thinking the clean white beds looked inviting.

But she had scant rest that night. She spent the long hours fighting bedbugs, ravenous little creatures she feared might injure her baby, so she stayed awake fending off the insects and watching her child. In the morning she cut some patterns for Mr. Schafer's wife as payment for her accomodations, then started with her models and her little girl into the country, enjoying the walk through the fresh morning air.

The nearest farmhouse was only a mile distant, but their family was large and they could not take boarders. Ellis sat under a tree and ate a lunch of homemade bread and milk, then started out again. But now the walking was no longer pleasant. There was not one friendly cloud to shield her from the scorching sun and her arms ached as though they would break from the weight of the baby. Each mile seemed longer and dustier and more painful. Occasionally she found an old gnarled tree with some shade where she could take refuge, but the trees seemed a great distance apart.

At last she reached another farmhouse, a cool inviting oasis set in the expanse of heat-shimmering fields. The Dubois family, after some consideration, agreed that their eldest daughter might learn the use of the models and charts in exchange for Ellis's room and board.

Ellis liked the Dubois family immensely, called them "noble and kindhearted people" and observed that they seemed "to be lavish without being extravagant, and order and cleanliness reigned supreme."[27]

The following day, Friday, the last day of August, Ellis faithfully tramped the countryside with her models, but was successful in disposing of only one.

Saturday she walked into Salem, posted a letter, and collected the remainder of her belongings, which she had left for safekeeping at the hotel.

Scarcely had I entered when a young lady whose acquaintance I had made there said to me, "Did you not say that you were from Utah?" I replied in the affirmative. "Anywhere near Brigham Young?" I answered, "Yes," again and began to fortify myself for the questions that I expected to follow, little dreaming what her next remark would be, when she said, "I suppose you know *he is dead.*"

For a moment I could not breathe, my heart gave a sudden bound and then stood still, but I said, "Oh, no, it cannot be true." But there was something in her manner that almost convinced me at once that it was too true. She said she thought there was no doubt, for it was published in all the reliable newspapers of the day, and brought them for me to read for myself.

Oh, what sad news. How sorrowful I feel to think I will never behold that noble man again in life. Little did I think when last we clasped hands and he said, "I say go, and God bless you," that I would touch that hand and hear that voice no more in this life. — How I long to be home among the Saints of God, how hard to be away at such a time. My heart mourns for him as a father, a benefactor, and a friend, and as one of the greatest prophets that ever lived upon the earth.[28]

The following week Ellis spent in teaching the Dubois daughter and in canvassing several times, but with no success. Several days she was kept indoors by rainy weather, and enjoyed hours spent reading and playing with Olea. On Sunday she attended a "darky" camp meeting. In her clear and descriptive language she described the experience:

The ride was delightful, the recent showers washed the dust from the grass and trees, making them look so fresh and beautiful. There was one feature that seemed so strange to me — look where I would, I could see no mountains. When in the city with brick wall towers on all sides, I do not miss them so much. But to see level land and sky meeting on all sides gives me a strange impression. The world seems so small without those inanimate monsters raising their snowcapped heads far into the sky.

Away out in the woods a small space had been cleared away, a stand erected, and seats arranged. Here were blacks and whites assembled, the colored to worship God in their peculiar way, the whites doubtless from curiosity and for pleasure. But instead of being amused I felt more to pity them, so earnest and zealous, but yet so far from the truth.[29]

Two days later Ellis took the boat back to Philadelphia, thanking the friends who had cared for her so well, who had come to love little Olea and shown them such kind attentions. At noon she reached Ingersol Street, weary and hungry. Two good letters from Milford awaited her—food for the soul. She felt refreshed from the change and ready to start again.

The days flew by with their usual frenzy, each hour crowded with many things to do. Ellis visited the Medical University, the greatest institution of its kind in America, and made "a flying visit" through the Alms House. "The varying phases of human expression seen in the insane department," she wrote, "will not soon be effaced from my memory."[30] She struggled through a week when she was sick with chills and a fever, but could not afford the luxury of going to bed. On September 22 she thought achingly of her youngest, little Burt, who turned three years old that day. More than half of his life had been lived with her absent, deprived of the care she longed to give him. Two days later, out walking with Olea, admiring the gorgeous Indian summer sunset, she took a misstep and fell, spraining her ankle. The baby escaped unhurt, but Ellis spent a sleepless night in frustration and pain. She could not afford such an embarrassing handicap right now!

The next day as she lay in her bed Mrs. Wilson entered the room with a visitor, a strange lady, following behind her. It took Ellis a second or two, then she knew. It could not be—but it was—Maggie! They fell into each other's arms, laughing and crying. Maggie had made it back at last. How good life was—how much they both had to live for, and now they could encourage each other and work together. What a gift this was to bless her last college days!

The weeks flew; two more months of college life had passed. She had less than four months left to go. Each day brought her nearer her goal and, to add to her pleasure, she received a tremendous surprise from Milford. He was soon to be admitted to the Utah bar. He had been studying law on his own, in secret, hoping to surprise Ellis in the spring. Perhaps he felt subtle pressure to achieve, to keep pace with Ellis, with these lovely, ambitious wives in his charge. Ellis looked upon it as a "glorious blessing", "to know that that noble loved one has at last entered a field wherein he will have full scope for the exercise of his rare and brilliant talents."[31]

On January 20, 1878, Ellis turned thirty-one years old. She was now at the age her own mother had been when she died, when mortal experience for her had ended. But life for Ellis was just beginning. She knew it; she felt the power deep inside. She felt an inner response, an eagerness sweep her being. Four days later she received the wonderful news that Milford had been admitted to the Salt Lake bar as an attorney and counselor at law.

On March 14, 1878, Ellis recorded simply: "Graduated from College of Medicine, Women's Medical College of Pennsylvania."[32] The plain straightforward statement; that was all. The emotion, the discipline had already been spent.

There were many black people at the graduation exercises that spring, and several Japanese in the audience, but no other Mormons. Ellis received the signal honor alone; the quiet mark of achievement following the years of struggle and turmoil. She had reached the goal, and she knew this achievement was only a plateau, a level along the path that would ever climb upward. Hadn't she always chosen the steep, rugged path?

Someone (probably her daughter Ellis) later placed these words from Emerson at the front of her journal as statement, as theme: "God offers to everyone his choice between truth and repose. Take which you please — you can never have both."[33] Ellis knew that; she had very few fears or uncertainties left. She had embraced her course with the strength and purity that had sung through her life from its earliest days. She was ready to climb the next mountain and discover the new horizons beyond.

7

Practicing Physician

Ellis was thirty-one years old. She had borne six children and buried two. She had completed a rigorous course of study and earned the title of M.D. She held the distinction of being the second woman doctor in all of Utah. She had proven that a woman could dream grand dreams and mould those dreams into reality.

Now she was going home with her new credentials and her new baby, and with new dreams shining behind her eyes. "It was a toilsome, long, and anxious journey," she wrote, "that trip home on a second class emigrant train with my ten-month-old and teething baby."[1] In a fever of longing Ellis formed her pent-up emotions into the expression of poetry.

> On! on we go with lightning speed,
> And yet the pace seems slow!
> I pass each mile with avid greed,
> What joys I soon will know.
> So soon to fold my treasures here
> Close to this beating heart,
> With boundless joy and welling tear,
> My wealth of love impart.[2]

"As we came near and I could begin to see the mountain peaks and the wonderful vales of my Western home, I seemed to be translated to a sacred shrine of peace."[3] To her delight and surprise Milford met the train at Ogden, bringing with him her darling baby boy—no longer a baby, but nearly four years old. He scarcely knew her. She pulled him forward with gentle hands. Here was the most vital place where she would have to start over again.

She returned to the dear little house where twelve years earlier she had come as a hopeful bride of nineteen. She was greeted warmly by family and loved ones, and by dozens of cherished neighbors and friends who openly rejoiced in her achievement. A few of her "professional brothers"[4] rallied round expressing their confidence in her skills by sending many of their female patients to her. She secretly confessed in her journal that she was not really anxious to engage in a busy practice immediately. Through the long years of discipline and deprivation she had looked forward to the joys of home, of being a mother, of spending her hours reacquainting herself with her children, pouring out that love she had pent up inside. But there existed a "burning need of financial help."[5]

Milford had his own dreams, and they were not concerned with financial gain. He was educated in several vital fields, but he never concentrated his energies on one purpose and his dreams had philanthropic overtones. He wanted to help the Saints, educate them, equip them to handle the problems of life. There was little money in such a course and he knew it. But there were other intrinsic attractions that drew him on. And the other wives—it was their turn now. Ellis knew how patiently they had stood back for her. It was time to return the favor, and Ellis gladly "came to the rescue of those dear ones who had done their very best" for her.[6]

The *Woman's Exponent* for May 15, 1878, carried an advertisement announcing that Dr. Ellis Shipp would begin practice with "special attention given to obstetrics, diseases of women, and minor surgery."[7] Ellis opened her office in the old Constitution Building and, seeking to be professional, waited patiently for business to develop. Meanwhile, on August 13 in the historian's office, she was officially set apart for her work and given a priesthood blessing. This was a sweet and strengthening experience for Ellis.

Romania Pratt and Maggie Shipp were both set apart by John Taylor, Martha Hughes Paul and Ellis R. Shipp by George Q. Cannon.

Since professional responsibilities were developing slowly, Ellis came up with a plan that pleased her immensely. She moved from the old home and established her family right by her office on Main Street. Thus began one of the happiest times of her life. She had the companionship of her children as well as their invaluable help. She was fulfilling functions as a mother and as a doctor simultaneously and neglecting nothing. Her medicine became very much a "family practice," her children not only cooperating but sacrificing that those in need might have their mother's aid.

In these early days Ellis also devised a plan for teaching women the art of nursing and obstetrics. Her school was advertised to run two terms of six months each, with five lessons per week. At the completion of the course a certificate of graduation would be presented to each student who successfully passed. The examinations Ellis drew up for her students were approved and supervised by the Salt Lake Board of Health.

The summer following her return to Zion, on Pioneer Day of 1879, Ellis's third little daughter was born. She named her Ellis — the third to bear that cherished family name. She would grow up to name her own daughter Ellis, to look more like her mother than the other girls, to bless and brighten the world with her beauty and spirit.

According to family records, the following November, just a few days after Thanksgiving, Burt Reynolds Shipp died. There is no mention of this in Ellis's notes or journals. She did not keep faithful journals during these active years — did not even record the births of the four children who came in this period of time. She was too busy making things happen, keeping things running; there was no time for the luxury of contemplation and record-keeping. In 1930 when she was eighty-three years old she wrote a nostalgic autobiography, but her daily journal ceases with her medical school graduation.

The death of Burt must have been a difficult blow. He was the baby she weaned and left in order to pursue her education, whose infant experiences she had been denied. For so long she had been forced to neglect him; now, just as she gained him back, he was snatched away.

But life must go on, and the work with it. Ellis knew by now how to handle grief, how to tuck it away, sanctified and private, to be justified in God's own way.

In August 1880 Milford left for Jefferson Medical College in Philadelphia. Maggie was also in Philadelphia, at Ellis's old place, completing her studies. But Milford could never restrict his efforts or attentions to the purely practical, physical plane. On October 9 he was set apart as a missionary. He could preach the gospel now, which is what he loved best.

Ellis recognized the extent of this quality in her husband. In an earlier letter, dated 1874, she told him: "Today I have imagined you preaching—How I should like to have heard you. Preaching is truly your forte. I think your talents are too precious, too great and rare to be spent in financial pursuits. Someone else should make the money and let you do the preaching."[8] Now Ellis was making those desired conditions come true.

Ellis's practice by now had become very busy and successful. She had been taught that, as a new physician, she should seek assistance and consultation from more practiced doctors. She did this and was rewarded not only by an increase in her own knowledge and skills, but in the confidence and support they gave her. Often these doctors would remark to the patient or those friends standing near her, "You need have no fears when this woman is near. She knows her business."[9]

Ellis's services to a woman in confinement included prenatal care, delivery of the child, "ten visits after the birth when she would bathe mother and infant, make the bed, and sometimes cook a bowl of gruel if the mother's appetite failed; in fact, she did anything she could do for the comfort and well-being of her patient. The price? Twenty-five dollars when it was convenient."[10]

Ellis was in all phases of her work a true professional. "We cannot give what we do not possess, nor teach what we do not know," she stated. "Therefore I read and studied, seeking the progressive truths of my profession that I might impart to others, never giving my mind a chance to grow dormant, to forget the delicate points which, when overlooked, might mean the loss of precious life."[11]

She was instructing others as well as practicing, and she looked upon teaching as a sacred obligation. She would only be satisfied when she felt she was giving her students her best. And where her patients were concerned she went even further. Fearlessly, with a prayer in her heart, she walked the ill-lighted streets of the city. She had no husband to encourage or accompany her. A ruffian may be hiding in some dark corner, but she carried her big medical bag, ready to strike in her own defense if necessary. Through blinding rain, deep snows, over steep muddy trails she hurried time and time again to the call of duty, never worrying if the patient could pay, if she herself were well or sick, if her children missed her, if she was tired and had a class to prepare for the morning. She could never turn down a call for help and her children, though small, respected her for it and sensed the special nature of the work their mother was doing.

She considered it her sacred obligation to pray unto God for his blessing in her work. "Pray in your soul," she taught, "as you hasten to your duty." She spoke from the depth of personal experience and commitment. "I sought my Father and my God! He it was who inspired me with the higher intelligence, helped me to know my duty in all of its details, enabled me to run and not be weary, to walk and not faint. And with these same principles I tutored all who sought usefulness, enabling them to usher a new life into this world — that life so precious to the suffering mother and most sublime in the sight of God. I never yet have been able to express my satisfaction in this part of my life work, for thus have I been enabled to give and give of my knowledge and yet have more remaining to give over and over again."[12]

Ellis was seeing this glorious part of her dream come true — she was giving, with more and more left to give. She was destroying pain and ignorance, serving and saving the lives of the people she loved. "I know 'twas not of me," she often testified, "but through the touch of One Divine, upon whose mighty arm I leaned."[13]

In March 1881 Ellis's Grandpa Hawley died. He had lived to

be seventy-eight years old, to come back to full active fellowship in the Church. That was great comfort to those who loved him well.

Eighteen-eighty two was a memorable year for Ellis and for the progress of the medical profession in Salt Lake. In the early spring Eliza R. Snow, Zina D. H. Young, Emmeline B. Wells, Jane S. Richards, and Drs. Romania B. Pratt and Ellen B. Ferguson approached the prophet, President John Taylor, in his office in the Gardo House. They had come to discuss their desire for a hospital, to present their arguments and possible plans.

President Taylor thought it a very ambitious undertaking. But at the same time he knew the strength of the women of Zion. In 1870 the Legislature had granted suffrage to the women of Utah. In 1872 the women had launched their own magazine called the *Woman's Exponent* that the sisters "might represent themselves and tell their own story."[14] Emmeline Wells, the current editor, was one of the ladies who importuned him now. In 1874 the Deseret Silk Industry was established, with "Aunt Zina," Brigham's wife, at its head. She organized and taught thousands of women all through the state. Two years later the women had proven their merit in a Church-wide movement to "save grain against a day of famine."[15] In this project quiet but forceful Emmeline had again been at the helm.

In 1880 President Taylor himself had called Eliza R. Snow Smith to be president of a newly created Central Relief Society Board. The abilities and the character of these women, and many of their peers, were overwhelming. And the need was most certainly there; it did not have to be proved. Eliza said to him now, her voice forceful, "There are women in the stakes of Zion whose lives are being sacrificed to this need. . . ."[16]

This would be a hospital where the priesthood could function, where blessings could be administered as well as medicines without the curiosity or hostility of the world. The Holy Cross Hospital, organized by Catholic Sisters, had been in operation since October 1875. Another facility was sadly needed. The group talked about it; they organized. They chose capable and dedicated leaders to head their board and committees, Ellis Shipp among them. Ellen B. Ferguson was appointed resident physician, Mary Ann McClean was chosen as matron, and two prominent male physicians, Seymour Young and W. F. Anderson, consented to join the visiting board.

Financing for the institution was arranged uniquely. On what was called "the cooperative principle" each adult member of the Church contributed one dollar per month to the sustenance of the hospital. This money would establish credit funds in the wards where local patients who could not pay for needed attention could come for help.

The Deseret Hospital opened July 17, 1882, "in a large two-story brick house on Fifth East Street a little below South Temple, which had just been vacated by the Sisters of the Holy Cross."[17] Wilford Woodruff, President of the Council of Twelve Apostles of the Church, opened the dedicatory service with prayer. Joseph F. Smith, second counselor to President Taylor, addressed the group and exhorted the women to "be diligent, exercise skill, pray for wisdom, but above all things remain sensitive to the whisperings of the Spirit to secure the blessing of your Heavenly Father in this labor of love."[18]

The officers were set apart and many donations were presented: bedding, cutlery, crockery, kitchen utensils, and money — which included a five-hundred-dollar check from Mayor Jennings. The sisters canned fruits and jellies, which they donated to the cause. Quarters of beef and venison, pigs, cows, and chickens — people opened their hearts and gave all they could.

A benefit concert was held in the tabernacle during which the building was lighted with eight electric lights, "the effect being most intensely beautiful."[19]

Maggie and Milford both graduated this same year; thus Maggie was able to participate with Ellis in the great events then occurring. As the year drew to a close, on November 30, Ellis's fifth son was born. She named him Ambrose Pare after the great surgeon. Ellis herself marveled at how she lived "the dual life of a mother and a conscientious obstetrician."[20] In May 1883, when he was not quite six months old, little Ambrose died. Ellis was thirty-six years old. She had two sons and two daughters left her. She had buried one daughter and three small sons.

In July 1884 the Deseret Hospital moved to a larger building on the corner of Second West and First North. The rooms were bright and airy and well arranged, with many large windows and a good ventilation system. Ellis, who had served on only a visiting basis, was now added to the executive board which managed the institution. Her work, along with that of her colleagues, was purely a labor of love. All time, all effort was strictly volunteer, with only the resident surgeon receiving remuneration. Yet still the hospital struggled financially.

At the beginning the fee was three dollars a week, which included room, board, and nursing care. The hospital had a capacity of between forty and fifty patients, but even increasing the fees to six dollars weekly, double the original amount, did not alleviate the financial pressures. Many of the patients treated were welfare cases. Some of the wealthier Latter-day Saints preferred personalized treatment in their own homes. Eliza R. Snow tried to clarify the situation. She stated in an issue of the *Exponent* that the hospital "was not a charitable institution. The founders wished it could be so, but that was impossible. The hospital was, rather, a benevolent institution" involving labor and sacrifice on the part of many whose sole motive was the "ameliorating of the condition of suffering humanity."[21]

The hospital provided a dimension beyond good medical care. Prayer services were held there twice a day, led by Bishop Tingey of the Seventeenth Ward who would leave his small cobbler's shop to perform the service. "At the sound of a little bell, blue-uniformed nurses, doctors, officers, and as many patients as could, gathered for spiritual communion. On Sundays a sacrament service was held, as in regular ward meetings."[22]

Ellis was spreading herself quite thin, with her teaching, her own practice, and her work at the hospital. And now another baby was on the way. On March 19, 1885, a small son was born. Ellis records very briefly: "In the course of another two years my sixth son, Paul Elbert, was born prematurely and lived but a few hours."[23]

During these years when Milford was immersed in his own projects or involved in schooling and missionary work, Ellis relied very heavily on her children. There was a spirit in her home that was very rare. Ellis pays a stirring tribute to her sons, Bard and Richard.

> If honors should ever come from the practice of my profession, my beloved sons should share them. They cared for my infants, kept our apartments in order, watched the telephone, carried the messages to me. On one momentous day, through the aid of these two alert boys I attended five maternity cases in 24 hours, all from first to last ending successfully. On returning from the last case, with a keen sense of satisfaction and sublimest gratitude, I found my beloved assistants still on the watchtower with everything ready for mother to find her needed rest. And while I slept behind locked doors, the entrance was guarded that I should not be disturbed.[24]

Her daughter Ellis recorded the time when she and her sister Olea helped their mother "toboggan" down the steep stairs, at night, on a bedpan. She was too sick to walk down the long flight alone. When she returned, Bard and Richard carried her back upstairs. "How many times," she states, "all hours of the night— mother arose from her own sickbed to go to administer aid to some woman in labor or take comfort to some patient not so sick as herself."[25]

On November 28, 1886, when she was only seven years old, young Ellis wrote this little letter to her mother, which Dr. Shipp preserved in what she called her "Sacred Box."

> Dear Mama, Olea and I are very lonely without you and I want you to come home right now. The boys left us all alone and let the fire go out and we put some coal in the fire stove and we made a nice fire and thought you were coming home. Good night from your kind and loving daughter, Ellis R. Shipp[26]

Ellis recalled further that another night when their mother did not come home and it grew later and later, she and Olea—five and seven years old—"climbed up on one of the three high front windows to watch to see if she were coming. We fell asleep leaning far out on the window ledge. The ZCMI night watchman saw us from across the street and came over, pulled us in, undressed us, and put us to bed. He told Mother the next morning that every step he crept up to grab us he held his breath, fearing that we would wake, wiggle ourselves off that second-story ledge, and fall to our death below."[27]

Dr. Shipp often reminded the kind night watchman to look out for her little girls as he went his rounds. He was happy to perform that service for her and would many times treat the girls with a piece of ZCMI's hardtack candy which he kept a supply of in his pocket.

About this time Ellis graduated to the luxury of a secondhand surrey and a good horse. In the mid-1880s Salt Lake City had a population of well over twenty thousand. The savings in time and convenience the buggy provided were phenomenal.

Young Ellis, precocious — determined like her mother — remembered hanging onto the back of that buggy and running along, sometimes for as much as a mile down South Temple Street, barefooted, waving her stockings and calling, "Mama, take me with you, take me with!"[28] One time she jumped onto the train her mother was boarding and as it moved along was lifted into her arms and cuddled there, gentle fingers brushing back her tangled hair. There were no harsh words, no spankings for her willful action. Her mother took her the thirty miles to answer the call to a surgery case, treasuring as much as the child those hours in the jostling train together.

One of Milford's far-flung ambitions was to "lay the foundation for a private hospital for neurotic women and those suffering from psychosis."[29] He had no funds with which to build or rent a building, so turned his own home into a temporary ward. The medical staff consisted of himself and his wives, Ellis and Maggie. There was much general interest and there were patients in plenty, but as often happened, Milford's timing was bad. "The Edmunds-Tucker Bill was like setting off a bomb under the whole structure."[30]

In 1882 the United States Congress had passed the *Edmunds Act*, setting up a commission to supervise elections in Utah, requiring voters to swear they were not engaged in plural marriage before they would be allowed the right to vote. Rudger Clawson was the first to be arrested, then others followed, including Ellis's younger brother, George. In 1885 President John Taylor delivered his last public address and went into hiding. Pressure on those in plural marriage increased dramatically. In 1887 the *Edmunds-Tucker*

Act was passed, dissolving the corporation of the Church and taking over Church property. Most of the plurally married went into hiding or on foreign missions, some choosing to colonize communities in Mexico and Canada. The Shipp families, like many others, were scattered. Milford left for England and Ellis was alone with her children.

She mentions nothing of this in her journal. The fear and pressure, her loneliness at the loss of Milford, can only be guessed at. About this time, however, Luella Young, wife of Brigham's son, John, and a former patient, urged Dr. Shipp to come to New York and attend her at the impending birth of her child. The temptation was too great for Ellis. Her boys were leaving for missions and this meant she could accompany them on the long journey. She needed a change in her life right then. She arranged for others to handle her calls and lectures, put her household effects under lock and key, turned in the horse, Old Dan, and the phaeton for tithing and the milk cow to pay their grocery bill. Then with all four of her beloved children she set out to face the new adventure.

Ellis mentioned how delightful her daughters were, "not only beautiful in face and mind, but so perfect in spirit, obedient, gentle, charming, and interesting."[31] She noticed the many admiring glances that followed wherever they happened to go. Olea was ten years old at the time and Ellis eight.

In Norfolk they boarded a steamer to New York and her children had their first view of the Atlantic Ocean. John W. Young met them at the wharf and escorted them to his gracious home on Sheepshead Bay. He and Luella, the expectant mother, had two other children. But that was far from the extent of the household they kept. They entertained frequent visitors from Salt Lake; Ellis and her four only added to the number. That first night at the full-length dining table Ellis met "C. W. Penrose, George F. Gibbs, C. W. Nibley and wife, Joseph Felt and wife and child, and a number of others."[32]

Soon after their arrival, her sons were required to leave for their fields of labor. Ellis had written her farewell poem to each, but it was hard as the moment approached to let go. These boys had been her mainstay, her companions; bright and devoted they had stood by her side. Now she watched them walk up the pathway together, tall in the evening shadows, laughing together, grasping a heavy basket between them. The basket was filled with flowers and fruit for their mother. Ellis beheld them with the perfect love of a mother's heart. "Their speaking eyes, their smiling lips, and every feature of their handsome beloved faces, expressed the pure love which human words can never tell. Oh, the joy in their beautiful remembrance."[33]

Ellis had arrived in good time before the expected confinement. She enjoyed the rest, the walks by the sea, boat rides on the bay, and carriage rides in the parks and city. She took occasional trips into New York where she visited hospitals and observed important operations. "So long as I am a practitioner of the healing art," she wrote, "I desire to keep pace with the onward move of this wonderful science of medicine."[34]

In early autumn after the baby was born and mother and daughter were fully recovered, Ellis spent several months in Philadelphia gaining hospital experience and doing postgraduate work. She remained there with her girls until just before Christmas, marveling at how pleasant, how comfortable, current conditions were, and wondering how she had endured all she suffered here before.

In March 1888 Ellis was chosen, along with other notable Utah women, to represent her state and her sisters at an International Council of Women in Washington, D.C. The Council, called by the National Woman Suffrage Association, was the first attempt "to unify the spirit and method of the world's organized womanhood," and marked an "important epoch in the progress of the woman cause."[35]

Fifty-three different organizations and seven nations were represented. Nearly one hundred reports on women's work were read, including one by Emily S. Richards entitled "Women's Associations in Utah," and one by Ellis on the care and training of children. The greatest women of the generation were gathered there, and Ellis made the intimate acquaintance of many; Susan B. Anthony, Elizabeth C. Stanton, Clara Barton, and "a host of others."[36] This was a highlight for Ellis, another plateau, a plane of service she had not anticipated.

Suddenly, in June 1888, Milford returned. The *Deseret News* of June 18 printed the following item:

DR. SHIPP SURRENDERS HIMSELF. This morning Dr. M. B. Shipp, who has been in England since 1887, but who recently returned, appeared at Marshall Dyer's office and stated that he understood there was an indictment pending against him for unlawful cohabitation and he wished to surrender himself. The amount of bond was fixed at $1,000. —During his stay in England he had unusual opportunity of giving lectures at the invitation of temperance people. In these he was permitted to branch off into descriptions of this country and its people together with their religious peculiarities. He is in excellent health."[37]

This act of Milford's was in keeping with both his principles and his nature. On September 18 he was sentenced to pay a fine of $65 and be imprisoned for seventy-five days, but some family records state that he spent six months in the Utah territorial penitentiary, where polygamists served their sentences. George Q. Cannon, former Senator, was serving time, too. Upon his release Milford stated that this imprisonment attested to his religious beliefs and to his honorable and sincere regard for womankind.

When Milford obtained his M.D. he never intended to practice medicine actively. His purpose was "to better prepare himself to write and edit a health magazine for the people, that they might better understand first aid, home nursing, and sanitation."[38] In this respect he shared Ellis's deep concerns. "That he buried several of his children in infancy and young childhood," his daughter Bardella wrote, "seemed to him so unnecessary."[39]

He and Ellis and Maggie all became doctors. Then when his money had run out and his properties were mortgaged, he struggled to provide some lesser opportunity for Lizzie and Mary, who were trained as nurses, partly by Ellis. In fact, Ellis trained seventeen of her relatives to become educated midwives! This number included, perhaps fittingly, her daughter Olea, who was born while she was attending medical school.

In 1888 Milford started *The Salt Lake Sanitarian*, a "Monthly Journal of Medicine and Surgery." Drs. Ellis and Maggie Shipp were editors and frequent contributors. Near the beginning of the magazine's run appears the following rationale for its creation.

It is with no little apprehension that we launch the "Sanitarian" upon an untried sea. The domain of medical journalism with us has not, hitherto, been invaded. To publish a journal of health, such as we contemplate, has received our careful deliberation—and we have often asked ourselves the question, can we present anything to the public that will be of interest and profit.[40]

There was much presented of interest to the public. The Shipp will prevailed over difficulties and brought forth a product of taste and value.

In September 1889 Ellis's last child was born. She named the little girl Nellie. Ellis was forty-two years old when Nellie was born. Her oldest son, Bard, was twenty-two and Ellis, her next youngest child living, was ten. She had lost two boys since Ellis's birth; had buried five of the ten children she had borne. Nellie was the last jewel to add to her string, one last little treasure from heaven to bless her life.

The following year the Deseret Hospital was forced to close. Its finances had been falling behind year by year. Eliza R. Snow, with her other responsibilities increasing, had "regretfully and lovingly" resigned.[41] It seemed the problems outstripped the means and solutions, and a "beautiful dream perished."[42] "God bless the memory of the Deseret Hospital,"[43] said Wilford Woodruff, President of the Church when its final closing came. He had asked God's blessing upon its opening not many years before. They had been full and beneficient years. Other ways now had to be found.

Ellis concentrated on her practice and her own private school and wrote long articles for the *Sanitarian*. The insignia of the magazine read: "Devoted to the prevention and cure of diseases and injuries, and the promulgation of the laws of health and life."[44] Ellis usually wrote about very practical subjects, such as the use of olive oil, hygiene of beds, and a series of articles entitled *Mother's Methods*. She was not without some degree of humor in her writing, as when she told the anecdote concerning the poet, Alexander Pope.

A lady once approached him leading by the hand a child two years of age. She wished to ask the learned man's advice as to when she should begin the training of her little son. After enquiring the age of the child he remarked: Madam, you are just two years too late![45]

But Ellis approached most of her subject matter with the intensity and expressiveness which was her nature.

Still the deleterious effects of dirty beds are inevitable and I do not think we go too far in saying that they obtund the naturally fastidious tastes of mankind, demoralize and debase the delicate instincts, produce and foster disease, and shut the door against the spirit of divinity! For "the spirit of God will not dwell in unclean tabernacles."[46]

Ellis's teachings were clear and practical, and often spiced with little nuggets of wisdom.

Mothers, don't forget to keep the baby's head cool and feet warm. Give abundance of pure air, after the first week take it out for a ride or walk every day, suitably clad for the weather and season. . . . Every act we perform leaves with the brain a tendency or desire to repeat itself. . . . [47]

On the subject of motherhood she naturally waxed eloquent.

Are not the mothers of every race and color the custodians of the physical development and health of their people? Upon them more than any one else depends the physical constitution of their children. — Ah! how few mothers realize the effect of their own mental condition upon the minds of their offspring. Long before many are aware does the little one partake of the feelings and sensations of the mother. How soon the little innocent face learns to smile when mamma smiles, to beam with joy and delight when she is happy, and look sad and try to wipe the tears away with its tiny hand when sadness and tears are on her face. And likewise when swayed by the stronger and more tempestuous emotions of anger, hate, or fear do these tender ones partake, to a very great extent, of the same sensation.[48]

Ellis was at home in this field; she reigned supreme as an intelligent, far-seeing, sacrificing mother and as a dedicated professional who was willing to do all within her power to educate and uplift others.

8

Teacher and Healer

Life was a thing of constant change; Ellis knew that. In 1891, ten years after her husband, Grandma Hawley died. Ellis let go, glad to think of her joining her loved ones. But there were other places where it was more painful to let go.

After three years the *Sanitarian* ran its course. Why did all good things have to end so soon? It was difficult to give so much of herself, her efforts, her energy, her heart's love, only to see the creation dissolve and perish. Other things were dissolving around her, too.

Maggie — sister-wife, kindred spirit — divorced their Bard after bearing nine of his children. What direct reasons or causes there were have not been recorded. Bard was in some ways a sombre, demanding, judgmental man. Ellis had always been devoted to him and had chosen to overlook, even deny, his faults and failings. For reasons of her own Maggie changed her allegiance. And, surprisingly, after her divorce, Maggie married again, this time a Church authority, Elder Brigham H. Roberts. She spent many happy, productive years as his wife. But the tie between Maggie and Ellis was never broken. They had suffered too much together, loved too well, shared too many dreams they still held in common.

There is an undated verse Ellis wrote entitled *My Spirit Sister* which expresses the depth of feeling she had for her sister-wives.

> Oh, methinks in worlds afar, sweet sister-spirit, mine,
> We knew and loved each other with tenderness divine;
> That hand in hand together we roamed elysian grove,
> Heart beating close to heart, with pure, supernal love.
>
> How infinite His wisdom — How great His goodness, too,
> That still we can together His wondrous work pursue;
> That we, congenial spirits, can labor in His cause,
> And gain eternal blessings, by living sacred laws.
>
> And when life's work is finished and self we've overcome,
> With affection undiminished, may we meet again at home.
> May our crowns of endless glory with unceasing lustre shine,
> As reward for this probation — Oh, sweet sister-spirit, mine.[1]

In 1893 the Women's Medical College of Pennsylvania invited Ellis to submit a paper. She called it a sketch and entitled it "Woman in Medicine." She began with a statement of basic philosophy.

> The profession of medicine of all others seems best adapted to the natural instincts and capabilities of woman. Her clear judgment and presence of mind in the face of great emergencies, her intuitive gentleness, tender sympathy, kindness, and patience, especially fit her for this responsible vocation. The inspiring cheerfulness of her spirit acts as an elixis to life, cheering the suffering ones along the pathway to health; even at times doing more good than medicine.[2]

She praised those pioneer spirits who broke the path.

> What do not we the younger daughters owe our mothers, the venerable pioneers in this worthy cause, who so courageously faced opposition and paved the way for co-education in the great science of medicine. These women, all so true and womanly, and yet so brave and faithful to the cause they so unflinchingly espoused, using all their energies to place woman upon an elevated platform that she with man might possess equal opportunities for gaining a knowledge of that profession for which she is by nature so truly qualified.[3]

She concluded by acknowledging the current women who so ably and nobly served in the field.

This noble corps of workers, though engaged in laborious professional work, oftentimes intermingled with the sacred duties of womanhood, retain their mental vigor, and a spirit of constant progression, ever ready with voice or pen or active service to do all philanthropic work, or favor the honored cause of woman's progress. Success and glory attend you — women doctors.[4]

She acquitted herself well and her reputation grew.

During this period Ellis was involved in the Utah Woman's Press Club and for a period of time was president, hosting many of the programs in her large main office, or in her new home at 75 Center Street. Her children remembered sitting on the floor watching and listening as the sisters bore their testimonies "and sometimes sang in tongues."[5] Not only the leaders of Mormondom were entertained by this gracious young woman doctor. Harriet Beecher Stowe, Clara Weeks Shaw, and others visited Ellis in her home and were impressed by her gentle yet powerful spirit.

Emmeline B. Wells was one of Ellis's dearest friends. Ellis praised her for exerting "a blessed influence for my progression along literary and other lines."[6] No one knew poetry better than Emmeline Wells, and no one could have a more sensitive heart. She found much of merit in Ellis's poems and urged her to organize them with view to publication.

It was Ellis's habit to write poems for her children, usually on special occasions: a birth, a parting, birthdays, and Christmases. She would also write verse for her friends when she felt it might serve to praise or sustain them. And sometimes, coming home from a late-night case, she would form some reflective lines, then come home and record them. One such poem came to her while walking back from over the Jordan River at midnight:

> Along the winding river by the road
> I turn my steps at midnight's silent hour,
> I lift my heart in thankfulness to God,
> There own his every great omniscient power.
>
> I feel his love in moonbeams' softening glow,
> And twinkling stars that gild the azure dome,
> I hear it in the river's ceaseless flow,
> I see it in the dashing water's foam.

Again I hear it in the quivering trees,
Perceive it in fragrant flower's breath,
I sense it in the sighing passing breeze,
In blessed life and even solemn death.[7]

Ellis was more of a pioneer than perhaps she knew. The quality of her nursing instruction was commendably high and so was
the quality of the young women her school attracted. Bellevue
Hospital and many other centers in the East were struggling to rid
the profession of the stereotype of the nurse who was often slov-
enly, even drunk, and who used foul language. A higher quality of
young woman was at last being attracted to the profession: "Hundreds of attractive young girls, immaculate and eager to please,
were replacing the 'Sairey Gamps' who had so long held sway."[8]

There were few prototypes of Dickens's unsavory character,
Sarah Gamp, among the Mormon women who were attracted to
nursing. Rather they were women who had long recognized the
need, who had suffered themselves from the ignorance around
them, who were willing to sacrifice, to go to great lengths that they
might bless their lives and the lives of their friends with this knowledge. Dr. Shipp's contribution spearheaded far beyond those
women who received her direct instruction, for each went back to
her own community and trained local women there, so the influence mushroomed. These women went forth armed with Ellis's excellent training and with the strength of her philosophy as well,
imbued with her burning belief that through service we overcome
self and find purpose and joy.

Old friends and true, dear friends though new,
Come join me on my natal day.
Through fifty years of hopes and fears,
Through all my earthly joys and tears,
You've been, with God, my stay.[9]

So read the invitation Ellis sent for her fiftieth birthday, her
jubilee celebration. Over sixty ladies responded and gathered in
her home at 75 Center Street. Among them were some of the leading lights of the day: Zina D. H. Young, M. Isabella Horne, Bath-
sheba W. Smith, Emmeline B. Wells, and Elmira S. Taylor. They
spent the evening in conversation and music and recitation of

original poems written in commemoration of the event by Emily Woodmansee, Emmeline Wells, Ruth May Fox, Lydia Alder, and Sarah Pearson. It was one of those rare, sweet moments in time when some of the fruits of her labors were gathered; a pausing to take stock, to refresh, to gain from the kindness of loved ones strength to go on.

Gifts were presented: a handsome chair from the Woman's Press Club and the Reaper's Club, and another from the ladies of the dear old Eleventh Ward. Delicious refreshments were served at seven, which included trays of tea for some of the aged ladies, who returned them to the kitchen in favor of cocoa and lemonade.

The *Young Woman's Journal*, which reported the event, printed two of the poems of tribute in its pages. Some lines from Emily Woodmansee's read:

> As one of your untiring friends,
> I greet you on this festive day;
> And certainly it seems to me,
> You're passing by victoriously
> The fiftieth milestone on your way.
>
> Sustained by God's assisting grace,
> You've run the half of life's hard race
> And made a record bright and clear;
> And surely now, from friends sincere,
> Congratulations are in place.
>
> However beautifully clear
> Or brightly blue the present sky,
> Full well I know in days gone by
> You've lived through trials oft severe
> That taxed, and proved your courage high.
>
> Praise well deserved is ne'er akin
> To compliments from flattery's lips;
> Much honor you have earned, I ween,
> And loving hearts reserve therein
> A place for Dr. Ellis Shipp.[10]

As reported in the *Journal*, "the hostess was becomingly arrayed in a handsome black silk gown with white roses as the only decoration, and carried off the honors of her half century with her accustomed ease and grace."[11]

At fifty Ellis was still young, as energetic as she had ever been, beautiful, clear-eyed, slender still, but with an added dimension that came from her inner power, the strides she had made in self-subjugation, the compassionate qualities that had become part of her.

Dr. Shipp had what her daughter called "a healthy respect for herself and her accomplishments."[12] In an undated letter to her daughter Ellis she said:

> I believe if I keep my office here I will never be without some practice—at least sufficient to make our living and it is much easier than housework and work in the garden—and I am fully convinced that I should not do drudgery, and that when we go home we must have good competent help, for it doesn't pay us to not be professional.[13]

Yet never did she express the slightest hesitation, the smallest degree of frustration or distaste for her traditional role as wife and mother.

> Some women want to be men. Some say, "Oh, if I had only been a boy." I never felt that way. I was always glad that I was a girl, a woman, a wife, a mother. This is our mission, the greatest work that we can perform in this life is to be true wives and faithful mothers. Greater joy could not be had. Nothing can ever compare with the joy we have in our offspring.[14]

Ellis knew whereof she spoke. She had experienced opportunity, power, position—the freedom and praise of a man's world. Thus her testimony was rich with the ring of authority.

Once again Milford was not present to share in her pleasure and celebration. He was serving a mission to the Southern states, proselyting in Kentucky and Virginia, doing genealogical work along the way. It is difficult to envision such a lifestyle, but many elements had combined to create the current circumstances, the separate lives she and Milford seemed to lead. She had adjusted through the years. Her work and her children had provided compensations. Her old need for Milford was there, but she safely disguised it, and went on with the work of living at hand.

Although the hospital was no longer in operation, the Relief Society organized a nursing school. Maggie—now Dr. Roberts, but affectionately known as "Dr. Maggie"—was selected to head the school. Ellis in time worked with her, coordinating classes for women in outlying areas who were not able to travel to Salt Lake for school. That same year, 1898, Ellis was chosen to serve on the Relief Society General Board, which position she held through 1907. Milford was on another mission—this time to England. Ellis was approaching a turning point in her life.

Years earlier Eliza R. Snow, whom she called her "beloved friend,"[15] had urged her to extend her help beyond the centers of Zion. In her autobiography Ellis quotes Eliza as saying, "There are so many doctors here in this center stake of Zion. How I wish you could extend your needful service to those in other lands."[16]

Ellis treasured up her words; she did not forget them. It would have been impossible at first to follow such counsel. But in 1899, as Ellis put it, "when my two beloved sons were husbands and fathers in comfortable homes and prospering financially, and my daughter Ellis was in her last year of college work at the University of Utah, I left with my Olea and my baby girl, Nellie, for old Mexico."[17]

Ellis didn't seem aware of the courage such a course would take. She simply went on her way, and success went with her. She set up classes in the major cities and attended to daily and nightly calls as well. She and her daughters were usually "comfortably housed with kind and noble people of our own faith."[18] But Ellis felt that some of her "greatest blessings came with the kind welcoming and great appreciation of the presiding officials and, indeed, the whole community."[19]

There are only the very scantiest records of Ellis's activities during the years 1899 to 1916 when she was traveling in Mexico, Canada, and the Western states conducting her classes. Her daughter Olea in June, 1947, wrote a longhand account of several pages, recounting stories of a few experiences they had shared. Other than this, there is almost nothing remaining, save an attempted chronology of the years which reads sporadically and records dates that in several places conflict with one another.

One characteristic occurrence took place in Juarez. While Ellis was in the midst of teaching a class, a man burst in the door. He was disheveled and covered with the dust and grime of travel. His eyes when he spoke were wild and his voice insistent. Would the lady doctor come with him to Garcia? There was a woman dying in childbirth. Would she come and save her?

It might seem like a simple request, but the road through the mountains was treacherous; few would risk it. The irony of the request touched Ellis's mind. Garcia had refused to send her any students. Their response had been that they did not need such services as she had to offer. Now this man had come requesting her aid, asking her to make the dangerous journey, yet admitting at the same time that he had found no one in all of Juarez who would risk their animals and lend him horse or wagon to carry her back with him. His own animal was spent and exhausted.

There was tense silence in the room, then little May Ferguson, daughter of Ellis's own Aunt Mary, rushed up to the door. "I'll find one," she cried. A few moments later she returned with a stout spring wagon. "There!" she exclaimed triumphantly. But what could they possibly find to pull it? Before they had time to stop her May had turned and was off again. They waited; bewildered, praying—wondering. Suddenly the man called out, "Look there! That's the bishop's prize black team coming down the street!" And it was little May who was driving them. He had just come from there himself and the bishop had told him, "Do you think I'd allow my thoroughbreds to go over that road and take such a beating?"

They were incredulous; how had May done it?

"Oh, I just went to the barn and started to harness them," she explained, "and turned to the bishop and said, 'I came for the horses. You think more of saving a life than these beautiful animals, don't you?'" Not giving him a chance to reply, she continued. "'Well, so do I. I'm going to save Betty's life. She's my girlfriend—we've played together all our lives, and I want to find her again when I go home.'" She turned, with the startled bishop staring after her, leading his two prize horses away. "'Well, thanks, Bishop Brown.'" May's eyes sparkled. "Off I drove, and here's your outfit," she concluded. "Here, let me help you up, Aunt Ellis."[20]

They drove away with everyone calling after, "God bless you and keep you safe. God help you reach Garcia in time."

The road was a nightmare, sliding and sloughing away in places, tipping drunkenly at a dozen different angles so that it was hard to keep all four wheels on firm surface at the same time.

There were moments of sheer panic when one of the horses stumbled or one of the wheels slipped dangerously near the edge and they found themselves looking down cliffs that fell to a thousand feet below. Over many of the rougher sections they got out of the wagon and walked, leading the horses, placing every foot slowly and carefully.

At one of the turns in the winding road they were suddenly halted by a sixteen-year-old boy, the sick girl's brother. He had brought a relay to take them the ten remaining miles. His eyes were dull with pain, and tears streamed down his cheeks. His sister had been in labor for three long days. He was afraid she would be dead before they arrived.

Soon after Ellis arrived on the scene she discovered the problem. There had been an obstruction which made the delivery impossible. "With prayerful use of the catheter and obstetrical instruments," as Olea put it—did Ellis ever perform her work without aid of prayer?—"a half hour found the woman and babe safe and well."[21]

A miracle; simply and deftly performed. The bishop of Garcia, they discovered, was the father of the girl. He stood now humbly and gratefully before the woman who had done what he considered impossible.

"Sister Shipp, we owe our daughter's life to you and science," he said. "And I know now, too, you are a woman of God. I didn't send any students, but next week you'll have ten of our best women. Our poor wives and mothers will never again be left at the mercy of ignorance."[22]

It was a miracle and Ellis knew it; she knew that her Father was with her in her work.

The last days of 1899 rolled away and the calendar turned smoothly to 1900—the dawning of a new century. Ellis was fifty-three years old. She stood on the threshhold, knowing she was facing a different world, a world that would see the fruits of her efforts and bring women opportunities and blessings of which they had little dreamed. She knew she had filled the mission of pioneer; she had laid the foundation for others to build on, planted for others to reap, and that made her happy. But her work was in no wise completed or done. There were too many women who still lacked knowledge, too many homes where ignorance still held sway. Her traveling schedule was rigorous and demanding, but oh, so rewarding. She had seen the light of hope and knowledge leap into these women's eyes—she had kindled it with her own hands. There were too many eyes still dull with fear and suffering, too many women and children who needed what she had to give.

In 1900 Bard was released from his British mission. His health would not permit him to continue in the work. He came home, he played with his grandchildren, tended the garden that was his pride, read a lot: Bard was always a reader. He advised his neighbors on medical matters, giving freely of wisdom and knowledge he had obtained.

That same year on the Burlington and Missouri River railroad line, a mile and a half east of the Scotts Bluff station, the surveyors discovered a lonely grave, an old pioneer grave with a weathered marker made from a wagon tire two inches wide. Cold-chiseled into the tire were the words: "Rebecca Winters, aged 50 years."[23] The grave lay directly in the railroad's right of way.

Mr. J. R. Phelan, superintendent of the division, sent inquiries to Salt Lake City concerning the grave. The descendants of Rebecca Winters came forward. Much correspondence was exchanged. The railroad adjusted its route to pass by the grave site and preserve it for generations to come as representative of the countless graves that dotted the prairie, lost both to loved ones and to history.

Ellis remembered that long-ago time when she stood by her father, eyes wide with wonder, holding the light while he chiseled out the name—Rebecca Winters—and made his quiet prophecy: "This shall be the means of identifying this grave in years to come." She remembered; and the memory brought mingled joy and pain. The children of Rebecca Winters remembered, too. They prepared a tombstone, which Mr. Phelan cooperated in erecting.

> The inscription illustrates the characteristic devotion of the Mormons to their faith and to those who die in it. On the east side of the stone are the words: "Rebecca Burdick, wife of Hiram Winters. She died a faithful Latter-day Saint, August 15, 1852, aged 50 years, while making that memorable journey across the plains to find a new home in the far distant Salt Lake valley. She gave her life for her faith, and her reward will be according to her works.

This monument was erected in 1902, her centennial year, by her numerous descendants in Utah." This verse then follows:

> And should we die before our journey's through
>> Happy day, all is well;
> We then are free from toil and sorrow, too.
>> With the just we shall dwell.

On the west side of the stone are the words: "Our beloved mother"; and lower down under a picture of the temple, "Salt Lake Temple." The word "Winters" is chiseled in the base of the monument on the west side and in the foundation, "Temple Granite." [24]

Ellis contributed her own monument. She called her poem "The Grave In The Desert." It is tribute not only to Rebecca Winters, but to her grandparents and her parents as well — to the sacred memory of all the unsung pioneers.

> On a lone and dreary prairie,
>> Near the banks of North Platte River,
> Pioneers in grief were camping,
>> Camping on the lonely prairie,
> For a noble, faithful mother
>> Had succumbed from dire privation,
> Had exhausted all her powers
>> And had passed from all her sorrows.
>
> Then her little daughter Helen
>> Wept with childish grief unbroken,
> Sobbed upon her father's bosom
>> While he held her closely folded
> To his heart with grief o'er-laden.
>> Wistfully I gazed upon her;
> Sympathetic tears in showers
>> Flowed with those of little Helen.
>
> For upon tomorrow's morning
>> We must hasten on our journey,
> Go without our playmate's mother;
>> Leave her buried on the prairie,
> Where no tender hand could scatter
>> Flowers of loving recollection; —
> Where fond tears could never water
>> Tender buds which here might blossom.
>
> But my grandsire, rich in wisdom,
>> He the counsellor and leader —

He the noble, honored captain —
    Could not deem it just to leave her
Thus without a slab or gravestone.
    Then he called my worthy father,
Who, with will and genius ready,
    Brought a cast-off wagon tire.

And upon it chiseled plainly,
    Just the name "Rebecca Winters,"
Then this tire round, unbroken,
    Like the love of those who left her,
As our monument — our token,
    Was secured by dext'rous working
Round about the stone and boulder,
    And the greensward smoothly moulded.

Then we passed upon our journey —
    Far away o'er hill and prairie,
Over bare and sandy desert,
    Over steep and shelving mountain,
Leaving her in death to slumber
    In her grave so still and lonely,
In the solitude of nature —
    In the presence of her Maker.

On we passed with prayers to heaven
    That this grave should be protected,
That the sod should stay unbroken,
    That this circling band of iron
Should remain where hands so willing
    Here had placed it mid their sighing,
That the spot of her interment,
    Might be found by those who followed.

Now, though years have flown — full forty,
    Since we left her on the prairie —
Comes a distant, far-off message:
    Close beside the North Platte River,
Has been found a grave still guarded
    By a tire of rusted iron,
And upon it, plainly graven,
    Honored name, "Rebecca Winters"!

Still legible the chiseled letters,
    Symbols formed by hands now folded
In the last, long sleep of mortals.
    With this message comes the query:

"Who was she, — Rebecca Winters?
    Pioneer?" Ah! truly was she!
Placed her all upon the altar,
    Gave her life for cause most worthy!

Then should we, the sons and daughters
    Of such mothers — Of such fathers
Give to them deserving honors
    For the hardships and privation,
For the trials they encountered,
    For self-sacrifice and patience
On that long, eventful journey
    To redeem the western desert! [25]

Somehow Ellis juggled it all together: local practice, local teaching — in her own school as well as the Relief Society's — work on the General Board and extensive travel. In the year 1901 alone, according to records, she visited Rexburg, Pocatello, and Soda Springs, Idaho; Mesa, Arizona; and parts of Oregon. There was one short outline of her travels in Idaho printed in the *Woman's Exponent*, graphic in detail and infused with the beauty of spirit and language that characterized Ellis:

> Here I am in the wonderful Snake River Valley with the famous Teton Peaks towering in the eastern sky, white with their ever-lasting mantle of snow. . . . Since leaving Salt Lake City one month ago, I have visited twenty-seven towns, holding three meetings in each. I have traveled two hundred and fifty miles by train and nearly five hundred by team, over hills and dales, through canyons and mountain gorges, over sagebrush plains and lava beds, along shady glens and fragrant meadows. . . . We have many ditches, creeks and canals to ford, sometimes the water coming into the wagon bed. . . . Many of the little towns are situated along the picturesque banks of the Snake River. . . . When the little towns and hamlets become large cities with towers and spires reaching heaven-ward, and the plains covered with extensive orchards, then we may expect a change in climate as we have found in our own loved Utah. [26]

Dr. Shipp spent part of the year 1902 in Mexico and part in Thatcher and Pima, Arizona, where she had the exciting adventure of driving back and forth from classes in a two-wheel cart drawn by an impetuous race horse. Although her schedule may have been crowded and demanding, Ellis made certain the women she taught were really learning. Once in Arizona, with a model pelvis to serve as example, Ellis lectured on the subject for over an hour, hardly stopping to catch her breath. Then she handed the pelvis to the stake Relief Society president and required her to lecture some in turn, repeating principles to see if she understood them. Then each woman in the room had to do the same before Dr. Shipp was satisfied with the session. The repetition as well as the opportunity of personal involvement helped solidify the information in her students' minds.

In May 1904 William Reynolds died at the age of seventy eight in Sanford, Colorado. He had been the last link to Ellis's past, to her childhood, to the memories of the mother she still adored. In 1899 she had paid him a visit, at the same time conducting classes in that area. This was her last experience with him, and she has left a record:

> When the parting time came I had a premonition that our next reunion would be in that "Better Land" where parting never comes again. How bitterly I wept as he clasped me in his arms, just as in the olden days when he would still my cries and repeat, "Don't cry, darling." This time how well I understood his comforting words and well knew his words would come true—"We would meet again." But not in this life.
>
> Although in those later years we were so far distant from each other our devotion for each other never wavered. I knew no child ever had a more tender, kind, and helpful father, one more faithful and mindful of a daughter's welfare, more exemplary and wise in his teachings, more lovingly true.
>
> I was far away when his call came, when the sad news reached me and I knew I was an orphan indeed! I was far from home and all my kindred—no comforting note could reach me, saving the echoings of memory: "Don't weep, my child, we shall meet again."[27]

In 1906 Olea married and lived in the home on Center Street. Three years earlier Ellis had purchased another property at 713 Second Avenue. She was meticulous in affairs of finance as in all others and worked diligently to repay debts as quickly as her means would provide. It was a joy for her to assist her children, to provide them with the beauties and comforts of life she had wanted for them those long years ago as she walked the elegant Philadelphia streets and sacrificed for just such a future.

In 1910 another dream of her life came true; a sensitive, private dream she had long cherished. A volume of her poetry was published by the Skelton Publishing Company in Salt Lake. She chose the title *Life Lines* and was honored with an introduction by Emmeline Wells in which she said, "The author has chosen for this book a peculiarly fitting title, that is depicted in vivid outline on the cover of the volume of poems, now to be launched forth into the world of letters."[28] The introduction goes on to praise the poems—their themes, their sensitive use of words. It concludes with the following paragraph:

> We commend "Life Lines" to the world, and especially to the people of these mountain valleys; to the Doctor's many, many friends, already familiar with her writings, commendation is quite unnecessary. We believe the book will be a blessing and inspiration to those into whose hands it may come, because of the spirit of love in which it is sent forth; and we would say, read and consider its value, and it will be more precious than rubies, for it will give you gems of thought for daily need and comfort.[29]

Life Lines contains nearly three hundred poems, an impressive number. Few people, even those who consider themselves poets, create that number of works during their lives. Not all of her verses would be considered poetically excellent or sound. But some are little masterpieces, and all portray an eloquence of emotion, a depth of perception and feeling worthy of the embodiment of expression.

On the title page of the book Ellis placed a quotation from Shakespeare:

> And this our life, exempt from public haunts,
> Finds tongues in trees, books in the running brooks,
> Sermons in stones, and good in everything.[30]

She dedicated the volume to her children and the depth of emotion in her words can still be felt.

> To my beloved children who through all their lives have been the strongest incentive to my best thought and endeavor: my purest, tenderest, truest joy, my highest inspiration, my lifeline linking with Eternity, these heart-throbs are lovingly dedicated by their mother.[31]

Following publication of her poems, in 1911 and 1912 Ellis traveled extensively in Canada. There were large communities of Latter-day Saints there and an abundance of work to be done. She was sixty-three years old but she hadn't slowed down yet. She knew how to push her own problems and sufferings aside. The young woman who in her twenties had been told by the doctors that her heart was skipping beats and she might not live much longer, had come home to bear five more children and fill her years with more service and accomplishment than half a dozen ordinary women.

In 1913 Nellie, her last, was married. Three years later, on May 5, 1916, Ellis and Milford celebrated their fiftieth wedding anniversary. There is no information concerning the occasion save the fact that it took place at 713 Second Avenue, the home Ellis had purchased thirteen years before. There was great satisfaction in reaching this milestone with Bard, in having him seated here by her side, in knowing that she had endured every trial and privation and could still adore and honor this companion of hers, this man she had loved and served all the days of her adult life. Honor, integrity, faithfulness, endurance — these were the attributes Ellis had clung to through the years — the strengths she had wished to incorporate into her being. They were part of her now, and their strength was felt in the countless lives that came under her influence.

Milford's time was short now, though Ellis didn't know it. On March 15, 1918, just twelve days after his eighty-second birthday, he died. Ellis, who had loved him when she was a child of twelve, was a young and still lovely seventy-one. She mourned him; no one could know how she mourned him. He was spirit of her spirit, soul of her soul, the light that had kept her going through hours of darkness, the faith that had helped her unlock her inner powers and find fulfillment of her dreams.

Milford was the father of thirty-six children. During his lifetime he had lived with six different wives, four under the sacred order of plural marriage. He had been sealed in the temple to four other women, given to him as "celestial wives." Throughout his life he had honored women and been an active supporter of women's rights, holding motherhood in sacred esteem and believing that a noble woman was capable of any high station to which she aspired. He had been possessed of intelligence, culture, and charm, and the powers of a natural orator. He had used the gifts of his life in service, filling eight separate missions for the Church, giving "eighteen years of the best years of his life in active service to his God in spreading the gospel of truth to those who were seeking it."[32] He died in the Forest Dale Ward, and a funeral service was held in the chapel there.

Perhaps the most fitting tribute to Milford which has been recorded lies in the words of the birthday letter Ellis wrote less than two weeks before his death.

> Emery, Emery County, Utah. March 3, 1918: My Dear Milford: —Please excuse this paper—it is not worthy [of] the cause it represents. I would not think a golden tissue what it should be, to do honor to you on this important and really wonderful occasion —your 82nd Anniversary! How little we thought in the early days that either one of us would get this far toward the centennial period of mortal life. Who knows but both of us may reach the one hundred mark! I can see you smile and shake your head—but really it might be so.
>
> How true it is that "our words and our deeds live after us"—I know that yours will—and best of all—live for the blessing of humanity. It seems to me that this thought ought to make you feel very happy. You must think of this today and of everything else that is bright and beautiful that can shed a ray of comfort and delight. Just think how happy I was when you told me of your love—in those dear old days in our own Pleasant Grove more than fifty years ago! Perhaps sometime, somewhere, we will again roam together in fair elysian fields when we are both immortalized, and have passed beyond all the struggles of vain mortality.
>
> I am with lovely people and have every comfort, I am working every day and trying to do all the good I can, and this gives me satisfaction, but there is ever a yearning and a longing for the beloved ones at home. How I would love to be with you today to help other loving ones do you honor. I surely hope it will be the very best birthday you have ever had—with more of the good things of life showered upon you—more kindness and consideration—*More Love!* More of the sweet, pure influences of the Holy Spirit whose joy and blessing far surpasseth what mortals can give, or human hearts can understand. I believe you have this nearly always, because you have lived for it, worked for it so long and

faithfully — but this day I pray it may fill your soul more abundantly — that a sweet calm and peace may abide with you now,
and evermore. [33]

Ellis, who had learned to stand alone — even when she hated
to do it, even though she may have longed for comfort and sustenance — turned her back on the past and tucked it away with her
treasures, and with her face to tomorrow walked on, alone.

9

The Love of a People

Ellis had unwillingly rounded another corner; life would never be the same for her without Bard in it. And she was taught that ever-recurring lesson that troubles never come one at a time; they come in batches. The same year she lost her husband she also lost her son. Milford Bard, her eldest, named for his father, died at the age of fifty-one. Her children were her brightest treasures; she clung to her children. Now, of the six sons she had borne, she had only one. One noble son, three lovely daughters. During the years to come she would build her life more and more around them, nurturing their children as they came, imbuing them with the intense beauty and strength of her own spirit.

The following year Ellis traveled to California, perhaps hoping in part to get away, keep busy, and not allow memories to fester, or any degree of self-pity to creep in. But as the years progressed she traveled less often, concentrating more time on her practice and teaching. She apparently owned several properties, including extensive shares in the North Antelope Mining Company, along with several of her children. It is interesting that as Milford's widow she received a small pension from the United States. The sum of twelve dollars was sent her monthly as pension for Milford's services as First Lieutenant in Utah's Black Hawk War.

Ellis was still as dedicated to her work as always. When she was called to go she dropped everything and went. "Do you have money to pay?" was never asked. If she was needed she would go, no matter what personal price she had to pay.

Her daughter Olea tells of one instance when Dr. Shipp went to treat a woman who lived west of town in a dirty little tumble-down shack. With her anesthetics and antiseptics she set to work and brought the new baby successfully into the world. She discovered that there were no clothes for either the mother or the child and looked around her for what resources might be available. The walls of the little hut had been covered with cheesecloth. Ellis "stripped the cloth off, put on a tub for a boiler, made a fire, washed, ironed, cut, sewed, and antisepticized all day. When she left, mother and babe were comfortable, clean, and safe — and clothed."[1]

This was common practice for Ellis. She left a long wake of women who blessed her name.

In 1926 Maggie Shipp Roberts died. It was one more letting-go for Ellis. She concentrated on her children more and more, especially Olea who was having problems. In a letter to her remaining son, Richard, she wrote: "My Beloved Son: My "ever faithful" — this is the name for you, my dear Richard, for you never fail me. I hope these words speak the volumes my heart cannot explain."[2] She went on to ask him to help his sister, visit her, sustain her in her time of trial, and ended with the plea, "Oh, my boy, what can we do for her?"[3]

She was the type of mother who was consumed with concern for her children, whose own sensitivities made their pains and troubles pierce with arrow sharpness through her heart. In a letter written to her daughter Ellis in 1917 she expressed this:

> My Beloved Daughter Ellis: — Could all my yearning desires and my fervent prayers for your happiness become living, breathing realities — then I am very sure my own precious lapchild would be a very happy girl. This birthday would then surely be the very brightest, happiest, most perfect one you have ever known — the cares and trials of life would all forgotten be — the perplexities and

worries all flown to the far winds—to no man's land—where no other heart could ever feel them as my darling has so oft in these last months and years. Oh my precious child, if only I could, how gladly would I shield you! . . .[4]

Ellis's correspondence during the 1930s is heavier than at any other time. She was not able to travel as freely as she once did and visit her scattered family. The great majority of her letters are directed to Ellis, her namesake, but many are to her grandchildren as well as her children. She still composed her annual Christmas poem and verses on birthdays and other occasions. Lines from one of her Christmas verses follow:

> May the peace of Christ our Savior,
> Shed its incense in each heart,
> For His love, above all others,
> Greatest blessings will impart.
> He hath made all nations kindred,
> By His sacrifice divine—
> Lightened oft life's weary burdens,
> Lifted even thine and mine.
> May His presence now at yuletide
> Every Christmas joy increase,
> Bringing hope, and faith unfailing,
> To thy heart and home, sweet peace.[5]

In January 1933, as she had her eighty-sixth birthday, Ellis composed a letter and addressed it to "my honored and beloved kindred." In it she expressed her love and gratitude for her children and grandchildren, her "deep admiration and reverence for such worthy representatives of a noble race of people.—Ah, how thankful and happy you must be in contemplating the life and works of your loved and honored progenitors. Truly you would naturally bend every effort of your being to follow in their illustrious footsteps, and I feel sure never pause to criticize unkindly."[6]

Ellis always believed the best of other people and, by holding them in high esteem, inspired them to attain their highest potential. Especially was this true with her own children. Every one obtained a college degree. Olea was talented musically, and all rose to lives of distinction and service.

In the year 1935 a singular honor came to Ellis. She was invited back to the Women's Medical College to be honored as their oldest living graduate. It was a wonderful experience for her from start to finish. On Sunday, June 2, she arrived in Washington and toured the city with her daughter Ellis and family. They crossed the new bridge to the Lincoln Memorial and attended services at a new LDS chapel where they heard J. Reuben Clark speak.

Monday, June 3 they visited the Capitol and met Chief Justice Hughes, toured the court chambers and observed the last session of the Court in its old chambers, which had been occupied since Lincoln's time. That same afternoon they attended a luncheon given in Ellis's honor by Alpha Epsilon Iota, the national women's medical sorority, of which she had been made an honorary member. The following morning they drove to Philadelphia.

Wednesday, June 5, was commencement day. Dean Martha Tracy met Dr. Shipp on the campus and took her on a tour of the school. Everyone was thrilled to have her visit, this gracious, quiet woman, still straight and slim, still with a light in her eye that excited attention and a warmth that drew others to her naturally.

They drove to the church where the exercises were to be held. Several reporters were there to photograph Dr. Shipp with Dean Tracy; movies were taken, which interested Ellis. The dean, dressed in cap and gown, with the doctor's robes upon her, led the march of the alumni. Ellis, all in white, walked with her. It was a lovely, solemn sight to those watching.

After the degrees were presented, Dean Tracy conferred on Dr. Ellis Shipp the gold medal awarded to those graduates of the college who had practiced medicine for over fifty years. As the medal was pinned on her, the whole group spontaneously arose — officials, students, and spectators together — applauding enthusiastically in her honor. It was the biggest demonstration of the day.

Ellis looked out over the sea of kind, friendly faces. No one could fathom the sensations of her heart. She had proven herself and come back with honors. The quiet little plural wife from Utah who had been told to go home and prepare to die, who had been advised to abort the child she carried, who had studied long hours alone in her attic room, defying both circumstances and tradition, stood before them now as a standard, a shining example of all that was best and noblest in their field, demonstrating the heights their profession could rise to when embraced by a woman of talent, dedication, and integrity.

A special luncheon followed the ceremonies. Ellis sat at the table of honor with the dean. Dr. Babbit, who had delivered the commencement address, was fascinated and asked the elderly doctor a myriad of questions. Ellis was beautiful still, although she was eighty-eight years old. Graciously she responded to his questions, telling him much of her early school days and her struggles at the college. He kept shaking his head and repeating over and over, "What a remarkable woman — what a remarkable woman!"[7]

In the quiet that followed all the formal celebrating, Ellis visited the old hospital, the old school, the house which had lodged her fifty long years ago. There were many memories here in the whispers and shadows. Even she looked back with some sense of awe. Had she really come so far from these trying beginnings? It had happened so simply, a step at a time, each new day of doing her best at whatever came to her. Now viewed with time's perspective, viewed as a whole, she could see some of the strength and beauty of her life's pattern. It was a wonderful realization to hold on to.

With her daughter to set the pace, to see to the details, Ellis extended her trip and visited New York: the ocean beach where "The Normandie" sat in dock, the Statue of Liberty, Trinity Church, Times Square, Wall Street, Broadway, and Radio City.

What a fascinating experience it was for her to sit through a gala presentation in Music Hall! Moving pictures were a wonder to her. The world had traveled such a long distance since she was a girl, since she sat huddled through a Pleasant Grove winter with nothing to eat but cornbread and beet sugar and nothing for light but homemade candles! Now there were such wonders as brilliant electric lights, steam heat — even gas heat in homes. There was the modern refrigerator to replace the old ice box, electric ranges to cook on, and vacuum machines. All these conveniences were a blessing to women. Occasionally Ellis wondered how different her own life might have been with the help of even some of these devices which the rising generation took so much for granted.

Travel and communication had become so easy. She thought of the many miles she had walked, never dreaming that automobile travel was in her future. And not only automobiles, but air travel, which was difficult for her mind to grasp. She had witnessed the horrors of a world war, demonstrating the awful and amazing things that could be done with technology. And what a difference the telephone made to medical practice. It seemed a world of magic and wonder to Ellis.

During her youth she had been sensitive to beauty and to music and had longed for their influence in her life. Now the radio and the phonograph brought instant fulfillment. Even common people had the means of surrounding themselves with beauty, comfort, and pleasure. During these same last years of her life another Mormon, Philo Farnsworth, a small-town boy from Beaver in southern Utah, was pioneering in a new field, developing the technology that would produce the television tube and open up one more plateau for human advancement.

But Ellis's life work was winding down. It was inevitable, though she hated to see it. And her cup of suffering was not yet full. In November of the following year, 1936, her son Richard died at the age of sixty-seven. She was bereft; all her sons were gone now. Not one was left to bless and support her old age. Of the ten children she had borne she had only three daughters: Olea, Ellis, and Nellie. But, oh what jewels, what faithful, sensitive girls they were!

Ellis's journal during these years is scanty and sporadic. An occasional entry reveals days that were difficult and lonely. On June 2, 1936, she wrote:

> Early morning. Work all done for the day — I mean the house-work. Bed made, house in order, breakfast over. *Now* alone — and quiet reigns! And now I must wait until my sweet comforter, my Nellie, comes to spend the day.[8]

And again, in November came a similar entry.

> It is now November and here alone in the Kimball Apartments I have passed a long, lonely day. Headache and heartache. No loving one has come to cheer. No sound of voice I love, so dear.[9]

And yet her need for independence was strong. Although she was living by now in a rented apartment, she wanted that freedom and privacy. She recorded her "innate desire" for "my *very own* home kept clean and liveable and truly comfortable, provided with all necessities bestowed through my faith and works—Blessed through my faith in *Heaven* in whom I trust so implicitly—That Gracious One who *never, no never forsakes* those in need—who are seeking to serve Him faithfully—To ever love and glorify His great and holy name."[10]

She paid tribute as she did all through her lifetime to that one very real and vital resource, the foundation of her own accomplishments and strengths: "He has all my mortal life kept me in His care. In my heartaches and many mortal sorrows when bereaved of my most priceless treasures He has sustained and comforted and given unto me the power to endure and feel He knows best."[11]

The nursing school Ellis established in 1878 had run continuously now for sixty years! It was a phenomenal, nearly unbelievable record. Now that, too, was drawing to an inevitable end. Over five hundred women had received certificates of graduation, and not one undeservedly. Dr. Ralph T. Richards wrote of Ellis:

> Doctor Ellis R. Shipp's great contribution to the welfare of the women of Utah and the Intermountain West was made by conducting systematic, thorough, and complete instruction classes in nursing and obstetrics. She gave them practical experience by taking them with her to her own cases. She was kind, considerate, and patient with her pupils, but she never gave a certificate of graduation to any student who did not have the mental and personal qualifications necessary to make a good practical nurse and midwife. [12]

Ellis saved the pictures of over three hundred of these girls and women she loved so well. They truly loved her in return, each one able to see the pure dedication and love that formed her strength.

In 1936 on her eighty-ninth birthday and again on her ninetieth birthday the following year, Ellis was honored at a Lion House luncheon, under the direction of the Yale camp of the Daughters of the Utah Pioneers. Many family members, close friends, and leaders in the medical profession gathered to reminisce and pay homage to her.

The Lion House and the Beehive House, its companion home, both held their own store of memories for Ellis. She had come to them as a young uncertain girl, with the promise of her tomorrows still hidden. Within their rooms she had spent many warm, enlightened hours as she felt her powers bloom and mature. In their parlors she had been courted by Milford. They had known her early hopes and prayers. The ghosts of her own girlhood walked there, as well as the powerful spirit of the man who had built them and brought her there, and stirred her faith and determination with his own.

In 1938, when Ellis was ninety-one, the Salt Lake Federation of Women's Clubs honored her with a place in the Women's Hall of Fame and presented her with a medal for her distinguished service.

Ellis had lived with her daughter Ellis off and on. Now it became again a necessity.

> I have experienced conditions the reason of which I cannot fully understand! The motive of my beloved daughter, Ellis, I know was to secure more comfortable conditions for me — than to be entirely alone through the nighttime. The doctors had, I suppose, diagnosed weak heart — the result of these conditions was to my beloved children a cause of worry which resulted in being bodily removed to my daughter's home with the *most truly kind intent*. Never could a mother have or appreciate more perfect kindness and more devoted and helpful and loving attention. For the sacred faithful care my soul is full of perfect gratitude. Never could there be a more devotedly kind child to a sick and sad mother than my beloved namesake, Ellis, has been to me.[13]

Ellis had always wanted to live a long life. But more than anything else she desired her life to be useful. She had been independent and self-sustaining since she was young. She had spent countless hours serving others; giving was a way of life with her. As a young wife struggling with pregnancies and poor health she had written: "Without health there is no usefulness, and without usefulness no happiness."[14] To live on for the mere sake of existence would be torture to Ellis. She expressed that sentiment in the following lines:

> To live kind Father, just
> While I can execute this trust

Of mortal life in usefulness,
So long as I can others bless,
    No longer do I ask.

When usefulness is o'er,
When I can help and soothe no more,
Nor ease the burdens others bear,
Nor mitigate their pain and care,
    I wish to go to Thee.

When that time comes, take me
To realms of immortality;
Renew my useful powers then,
So I can live and work again,
    For that would Heaven be![15]

On January 20, 1939, Ellis celebrated her ninety-second birthday. A few days later she began to fail. The last days of her life were spent moving in and out of consciousness, with her beloved children hovering near. Some of her last semiconscious messages were recorded; some very beautiful in expression were lost.

"I am going home," she whispered, "I am going so easy, nobody knows I have left."[16]

At several points she seemed to be speaking to her children: "Please don't suffer — any of you. Be enthusiastic and kind, and be gentle."[17] At other times she was communicating with those beyond.

Her spirit took flight on January 31. A granddaughter, home from her secretarial day's work, found her, in her last hour, talking to her children and thought her words so beautiful that she took them down in shorthand. Her last recorded words were:

> I am glad to see them. I haven't been with them for a long time. Please let me go on. — Oh, the beautiful mountains — I just love the mountains. There is a rosebush just beyond. I will send you flowers when I get on. Be kind and gentle. I pray the Lord to bless everybody, in the name of Jesus.[18]

All human beings are expendable surely, but some leave a greater emptiness when they go; their uniqueness cannot too easily be copied or compensated for. So it was with Ellis Shipp. There were literally thousands of people who felt a loss, an emptiness when they learned that the brightness and warmth of her spirit were no longer here. From simple women living in small Mexican villages whose struggles would never again be quite so severe, to the refined and educated women who had partaken of the beauty and wisdom of her mind, her influence would live actively on.

Her funeral services were held in the Yale Ward chapel on Sunday, February 5, 1939, at 1:00 P.M. Hundreds of humble and prominent people gathered to pay homage to her name. Those participating in the services included such notable leaders as Annie Wells Cannon, Ruth May Fox, Levi Edgar Young, and George Albert Smith. There were several vocal solos including "O My Father," that glorious expression of Mormon doctrine written by Eliza R. Snow who had been Ellis's friend, who had urged her to develop her gifts and talents and use them to bless her fellowmen.

Annie Wells Cannon was one of the speakers. She said in part:

> To have lived almost a century and then to quietly fold your hands and close your eyes and know that the Lord has called you home after having met all the vicissitudes of life with such courage as did Ellis Shipp is indeed the end of a perfect day.
>
> My first vivid impression of Dr. Ellis was shortly after her return from medical college in Philadelphia. I saw her in a room where one lady suffered and was in pain. She was beautiful, graceful, and calm and more than that, gentle and helpful. Into that room as she entered seemed to come a spirit of hope, comfort, and cheer. Always have I noticed these characteristics, not only in her professional career but her social life as well.
>
> To my sainted mother she was one of the dearest of friends. Let mother in her own words tell you this, for among the poems I found these lines to Ellis: "I count thy friendship as a precious boon. Indeed, it has been very dear to me. Among the many, many I have known, none have been truer or more sweet than thee."
>
> I never knew more devoted mother or truer friend. I loved her not alone for her high qualities of mind and heart, but her gentle spirit and pleasant ways. Her children and her children's children will always be proud to cherish her memory and fear not, but that in her Father's realm she will find peace, happiness, and progression. [19]

Levi Edgar Young, son of Dr. Seymour B. Young, friend and professional associate of Ellis's, was also one of the speakers that day. He paid humble tribute to both his father and Dr. Shipp for the courageous, brilliant work they had performed for others. George Albert Smith, one of the Apostles of the Mormon church who in 1945 would become its prophet, delivered the main funeral sermon that day. Excepts from the stirring tributes he paid her follow:

> There is a spirit in man, the inspiration of the Almighty given to understand. This good woman believed that, and she sought the Father's will in the duties of life and responsibilities. The result was that she achieved under the inspiration of that spirit many things that could not have been accomplished had she depended upon herself. Thousands bless her memory because of the work she has accomplished, her unselfish work. Today if we had the record before us, we would find the names of many of the illustrious men and women of this Church who came into being and first breathed the breath of life while this good woman attended.
>
> She has always been faithful. The Church of Jesus Christ of Latter-day Saints meant to her what it ought to mean to all its members — an opportunity for service, a stepping-stone to higher and more glorious opportunity and experience.
>
> We expect many things of strong, vigorous stalwart men in the march of time, but to few women has come the courage and fortitude and the determination to carry on amidst the difficulties and discouragements that we meet in our life here. This good woman has set us a wonderful example; and it seemed to me that no matter how old she became, year after year added to her treasure, and she was all the more determined to do the things that she thought our Heavenly Father would have her do.
>
> With all my heart I congratulate these who have descended through this good woman and can say to you, the best blood of the world flows in your veins. Her children, her descendants — she has lived for you. No more perfectly could one live than this woman has lived for those who have come after her. By so living you will have the happiness she has had, the assurance she has had, the satisfaction and joy she has had.
>
> Her joy has only just begun, for in the kingdom of our Lord and in the companionship of the best men and women that have ever lived she will find herself received with gladness and with acclaim. . . .[20]

Ellis was buried in City Cemetery. A granddaughter who came from far away at the time of her death, thought Ellis so beautiful after she died that she took a picture which her family placed near the great white throne at the cemetery — a monument to her "life of beauty and great service."[21]

The *Relief Society Magazine* printed an article at her death which reads in part:

> Dr. Shipp was one of Utah's most remarkable and noteworthy women; her long life one of unselfish service and devotion to her family, her friends, and humanity. Hers was no flower-strewn pathway; yet, from the beginning to the end it was an unfaltering course that led to a goal of achievement.
>
> Dr. Shipp was an ardent student, possessed of many natural gifts and charm of person, and found happiness in intellectual pursuits. She was a devoted mother and desired beyond almost anything to afford opportunities for her children. Her family and loved ones are rich beyond words in a heritage of loving service and sublime faith. [22]

The newspaper account at her passing read:

> One of Utah's most famous women, a medical practitioner here for sixty years, Dr. Ellis Reynolds Shipp succumbed to a heart attack Tuesday at the home of her daughter, Mrs. Ellis S. Musser. She was known throughout the state, held in deepest affection.
>
> Dr. Shipp's life was one of service. From the very hour of her birth she played a role in the dramatic story of the founding of Utah. [23]

The account goes on to recall her many triumphs and contributions and then states:

> These are only highlights in a career filled with achievement. She long since has become a famous personage in state and nation. Many professional societies have honored her with membership and other distinctions. — Active in the LDS Church and a member of the General Board of the Relief Society, she had played a large part in the development of its social services. She was a devoted mother and homemaker. She is survived by three daughters, 38 grandchildren, 25 great-grandchildren and four great-great-grandchildren.
>
> Dr. Shipp was a greatly needed force in early days here. Hers was a blessed service wherever she went. She won the enduring love of a whole people. She never lost the spirit of her calling, keeping alive the vision of a pioneer, seeking constantly new adventures in her profession, and exploring every avenue to progress.
>
> God, rest the dauntless soul. Her memory will long be cherished. [24]

The tributes to Dr. Shipp poured in. Just a few must serve as representative of the whole. In a letter to her daughter Ellis, written shortly after her death, Dr. Wilkie H. Blood, a Salt Lake physician, called Dr. Shipp "our outstanding woman of the last hundred years." He added, "I believe it will be another hundred years before Utah produces another woman whose service to mankind exceeds that which she has rendered."[25]

Dr. Ralph T. Richards, a Salt Lake surgeon, in his book *Of Medicine, Hospitals and Doctors* also comments on Dr. Shipp's long years as a physician and teacher and concludes, "The West owes her debt of gratitude."[26] In a *Deseret News* article dated November 10, 1932, Dr. Richards had also stated: "No one did more toward solving this problem [medical training and aid among Mormon women] than Dr. Ellis R. Shipp, Utah's Grand Old Lady! Unquestionably the outstanding woman of her time."[27]

Ellis brought more than six thousand babies into the world and lost only one mother, in a case where she was called to assist too late. It is nearly impossible to grasp such a record in terms of the individual experiences it encompassed. Ellis herself commented on it:

> Reverently unto God I give my gratitude for the successful practice of medicine in its many branches for the span of more than fifty years. For more than six thousand times have I felt the exquisite bliss of seeing the mother's smile when for the first time she clasped her treasure in her arms.[28]

Never did Ellis lose that sense of awe, a respect for the sacred nature of the work in which she participated. This respect, this dedication, was prime with her. She kept careful and accurate account books through the sixty years of her practice and there were thousands of dollars owing her. With a gentleness in her eyes she told her children, "When people have sickness they are having trouble enough; they should not be burdened with a single thought of debt. I want these books burned."[29]

Tributes came from not only the high and influential, and not only during the brief period of remembrance that followed her death. For years to come whenever medicine was mentioned — in book, in article, in conversation — her name would arise and be gratefully recognized and acknowledged.

Ellis Musser envisioned and brought into reality one of the most fitting tributes to her mother. Working with other women who loved Ellis, she organized and put together a special room in the Pioneer Memorial Museum dedicated solely to Dr. Shipp and her work. There, surrounded by her awards and diplomas, family and personal heirlooms, her likeness stands. She holds a baby in one arm, her bag in another. There is more than just beautiful symbolism there. She made her amazing dual life work on a practical basis and her role as mother, as nurturer of children, extended beyond her own few.

Fifteen years after Ellis's death the institution first called Brigham Young Academy and founded by that splendid leader of men, Karl G. Maeser—the humble teacher she had loved as a girl—honored her in a marvelous manner. Under the inspired leadership of Ernest L. Wilkinson, Brigham Young University had completed a large complex of dormitories to be used as women's housing. They were given the title of *Heritage Halls* and each unit was assigned the name of an outstanding woman, one who could be held up as an example for girls of all ages and times.

The names of the women chosen were impressive: Lucy Mack Smith, Eliza R. Snow, Emmeline B. Wells, Mary Fielding Smith, and Anna Meith Maeser. Ellis Reynolds Shipp's name was among them. A beautiful biography of her life was prepared and given. And with his inspired perception President Wilkinson made the following statements:

> It is a most joyous event because it gives us opportunity in a small measure to express gratitude, and provides occasion to be mindful of those who have labored that we might harvest, suffered that we might enjoy, and guided that we might follow.
>
> One group consists of sixteen glorious women for whom sixteen new group-living apartment buildings on campus are named. They include poetesses, legislators, leaders of women, artists, musicians, physicians, church workers, and women in many other roles, but none regarded any accomplishment higher than the calling of mother. Indeed, some are honored principally because of their exceptional examples as mothers. Although three were childless, they devoted their lives to the service of children, and no appellation in their honor was applied more or with deeper significance that the word "mother." The thirteen remaining each gave birth to an average of nine children, or 117 children in all.
>
> That their unselfish obedience to the divine command to "multiply and replenish the earth" did not impair their health nor shorten their lives is shown by the fact that they lived all the way

from 66 to 100 full and eventful years. Present and future generations will call their names blessed for the most precious gift of all —
the gift of life. [31]

Most fitting of all are the tributes given by Ellis's children,
those choice spirits to whom she had given the gift of life, who
knew and loved her most intimately, whose support and association she considered as the brightest blessings of her life.

Her daughter Ellis, who seems to have inherited some of her
beauty of expression, paid this sensitive tribute to her mother:

> Mother, I wish I could kneel at your feet today and look into
> your beautiful eyes, as deep as wells, as piercing as an arrow, as
> tender as a wild rose petal, and caress your hands, those magic
> hands. Eight times you have come to my bed to bring me safely
> through the "valley of shadow." You always knew just how to hold
> my back so it wouldn't hurt so much, and no matter how your own
> back might have been aching — it wasn't too much to give all of
> your strength to me.
>
> Do you remember the night you surprised us with an ivy-
> twined mantle which served for a Christmas tree? And then the
> lines you wrote:

> I twined a wreath while others slept,
> An ivy wreath. I worked and wept,
> It was not for the bonny bride,
> This verdant wreath at Christmas tide.
> It was not for the sombre bier,
> This ivy wreath and briny tear,
> It was for love, devotion true,
> Beloved ones, I twined for you.

> To my mind comes the financial struggle life has always been
> to you. How many times you have come home, your arms full of
> butter, eggs, chickens — the only pay you had received for your
> services. Your love of beauty; the world held nothing unsightly
> for you.
>
> And now I must close my task, faces fade away, but the face
> shining on me like a heavenly light that remains. My lamp burns
> low and I have written far into the night, but thy dear presence
> bears me company.
>
> Oh, mother, oh my soul. So may thy face be by me when I
> close my life. So may I, when realities are melting from me, like
> the shadows which I can now dismiss, still find thee near me, point-
> ing upward. [32]

Olea, Ellis's oldest daughter, wrote of her mother: "Is there an end to the marvels you can tell about Mother? Love — endurance — sacrifice. She had absolutely *conquered herself*. Her thought was for humanity — for you — what would *you* like? What do *you* need?"[33]

To overcome all her inner weakness, to conquer herself, to live for others — that had always been Ellis's goal. She had reached the desired plateaus, she had surpassed them, she had learned how to "give all of her strength" to others.

Ellis came to live the ideals she expressed in these lines from her poem entitled "Love Divine."

> And if a heart is sore with sting
> From slight or words unkind,
> May I the balm of solace bring
> Their wounds to soothe and bind.
> Oh, help me love humanity,
> And all its virtues see,
> For those who love most tenderly
> Are surely most like Thee. [34]

And she did truly love humanity, as is typified in this story:

A guide was taking a group of tourists through the Daughters of Pioneers Museum on Upper Main Street in Salt Lake City. When they reached the Dr. Ellis R. Shipp Room they saw a woman there, weeping. The guide went to her and said, "Are you sick? Can I do anything for you?" "Oh no," the woman wailed, "I'm all right. I'm just crying out my love for Doctor Shipp.

"Before I went to her class we were so poor, my children went hungry. Mothers and newborn babies were dying all around me. I thought if I could just study in Doctor Shipp's class and become a nurse and midwife, I could help my family and do some good in the world.

"I talked it over with my folks but they said, 'Why, you can't do that. It costs fifty dollars. You haven't any money. Besides, you have a crying baby in your arms, who'll take care of that?' But I wanted to go so badly. I couldn't forget it. At last I went to see Doctor Shipp.

"She put her arm around me and said, 'Of course you can come. You don't need any money. Come, I'll help you.' And we went. And she held my squirming baby on her lap while she lectured to us so I could take notes.

"I never paid her a cent, not even eggs. I was a new convert to the Church from Germany and could hardly understand or speak English. She was so patient, spelling out words for us and telling us what they meant. I helped bring a lot of babies into the world after I got through. Oh, how I loved her!"[30]

Ellis Shipp closed her own life story with the following prayer:

Great minds are they who suffer not in vain. Oh, I would hope I have suffered not in vain. If it is wondrous true, we have suffered not in vain. I do not feel my spirit great. But oh, I have suffered— and I pray it has never been in vain.[35]

Chapter References

Chapter 1

1. Sarah Ellis Hawley Pearson, "A Sketch of Our Beloved and Honored Pioneers of the Hawley Family," pp. 4–5; Ellis Reynolds Shipp Manuscript Collection, Utah State Historical Society, Salt Lake City, Utah.

2. Ellis Reynolds Shipp, "Autobiography of 1930," pp. 1–2; Shipp Manuscript Collection.

3. Ibid., p. 1.

4. Ibid., p. 2.

5. Ibid.

6. Pearson, p. 9.

7. Shipp, "Autobiography of 1930," pp. 4–7.

8. Ibid., p. 6.

9. Ibid.

10. Pearson, p. 10.

11. Shipp, "Autobiography of 1930," pp. 11–12.

12. Suzanna Mae Clark Grua, *Brief History of Pleasant Grove, Utah* (n.p., n.d.), p. 21.

13. Lucile Harvey Walker and Fern Eyring Smith, "Pleasant Grove," p. 179; Manuscript collection, Pleasant Grove Public Library, Pleasant Grove, Utah.

14. Shipp, "Autobiography of 1930," p. 15.

15. Ibid., p. 13.

16. Ibid., p. 14.

17. Ibid., p. 17.

18. Ibid., p. 14.

19. Ibid.

20. Ibid., p. 13.

21. Ibid., p. 19.

22. Ibid., p. 22.

23. Ibid.

24. Ibid.

25. Ibid., pp. 16–17.

26. Ibid., p. 26.

27. Ibid., p. 16.

28. Ibid., p. 15.

Chapter 2

1. Ellis Reynolds Shipp, "Autobiography of 1930," p. 27.
2. Ibid.
3. Ibid., p. 26.
4. Ibid., p. 27.
5. Ibid., p. 28.
6. Ellis Reynolds Shipp, "Early Autobiography and Diary," pp. 3–4; Shipp Manuscript Collection.
7. Ibid., p. 4.
8. Ibid., p. 23.
9. Shipp, "Autobiography of 1930," p. 19.
10. Ibid.
11. Ibid.
12. Ibid., pp. 22–24.
13. Ibid., p. 23.
14. Sarah Ellis Hawley Pearson, "A Sketch of Our Beloved and Honored Pioneers of the Hawley Family," p. 14.
15. Shipp, "Autobiography of 1930," p. 23.
16. Shipp, "Early Autobiography and Diary," pp. 5–6.
17. Shipp, "Autobiography of 1930," p. 23.
18. Shipp, "Early Autobiography and Diary," p. 6.
19. Ibid.
20. Ibid.
21. Shipp, "Autobiography of 1930," p. 29.
22. Shipp, "Early Autobiography and Diary," p. 6.
23. Shipp, "Autobiography of 1930," p. 24.
24. Ibid., p. 26.
25. Shipp, "Early Autobiography and Diary," p. 9.
26. Ibid.
27. Nellie Shipp McKinney, "Historical Sketch of Milford Bard Shipp, p. 3; Shipp Manuscript Collection.
28. Shipp, "Early Autobiography and Diary," p. 10.
29. Ibid.
30. Ibid., p. 11.
31. Ibid.
32. Ibid., p. 12.
33. Ibid.
34. Ibid., p. 14.
35. Ibid.
36. Ibid.
37. Ibid.
38. Shipp, "Autobiography of 1930," p. 29.

39. Pearson, p. 14.

40. Shipp, "Early Autobiography and Diary," p. 16.

41. Ibid.

42. Shipp, "Autobiography of 1930," p. 29.

43. Shipp, "Early Autobiography and Diary," p. 16.

44. Ibid., p. 18.

Chapter 3

1. Ellis Reynolds Shipp, "Autobiography of 1930," p. 31.

2. Ibid.

3. Ellis Reynolds Shipp, "Early Autobiography and Diary," p. 21.

4. Ibid.

5. Ibid., pp. 21−22.

6. Ibid., p. 22.

7. Ibid., p. 23.

8. Ibid., pp. 23−24.

9. Ibid., p. 24.

10. Ibid., p. 25.

11. Ibid., p. 26.

12. Shipp, "Autobiography of 1930," p. 32.

13. Ibid., p. 34.

14. Ibid.

15. Ibid., p. 31.

16. Alma P. Burton, *Karl G. Maeser, Mormon Educator* (Salt Lake City: Deseret Book Company, 1953), pp. 17−18.

17. Shipp, "Autobiography of 1930," p. 34.

18. Ibid.

19. Ibid.

20. Ibid.

21. Ibid., p. 35.

22. Ibid.

23. Ibid., p. 31.

24. Ibid., p. 32.

25. Ibid., p. 33.

26. Ibid.

27. Ibid.

28. Shipp, "Early Autobiography and Diary," p. 27.

29. Ibid., p. 28.

30. Shipp, "Autobiography of 1930," p. 32.

31. Ibid., pp. 32–33.
32. Shipp, "Early Autobiography and Diary," pp. 28–29.
33. Ibid., p. 30.
34. Ibid.
35. Ibid.
36. Ibid., p. 31.
37. Ibid.
38. Ibid., pp. 31–32.
39. Ibid., p. 32.
40. Ibid., p. 33.
41. Ibid.
42. Ibid.
43. Ibid., p. 34.
44. Ibid., p. 35.
45. Ibid., p. 36.
46. Ibid.
47. Ibid.
48. Ibid., p. 35.
49. Ibid.
50. Ibid., p. 37.
51. Ibid.
52. Ibid., p. 38.
53. Ibid.
54. Ibid.

Chapter 4

1. Ellis Reynolds Shipp, "Early Autobiography and Diary," p. 36.
2. Ibid., p. 37.
3. Ibid.
4. Ibid., p. 38.
5. Ibid.
6. Ibid.
7. Ibid., p. 39.
8. Ibid.
9. Ibid.
10. Ibid., p. 40.
11. Ibid.
12. Ibid.

13. Ibid., p. 42.

14. Ibid., p. 38.

15. Ibid.

16. Ibid., pp. 42–43.

17. Sarah Ellis Hawley Pearson, "A Sketch of Our Beloved and Honored Pioneers of the Hawley Family," pp. 18–19.

18. Shipp, "Early Autobiography and Diary," p. 45.

19. Ibid.

20. Ibid.

21. Ibid.

22. Ibid., pp. 46–47.

23. Ibid., p. 47.

24. Ellis Reynolds Shipp, "Autobiography of 1930," p. 48.

25. *Discourses of Brigham Young,* sel. John A. Widtsoe (Salt Lake City: Deseret Book Company, 1961), pp. 155, 291, 293.

26. Nellie Shipp McKinney, "Historical Sketch of Milford Bard Shipp," pp. 3–4.

27. Shipp, "Early Autobiography and Diary," p. 42.

28. Ibid., p. 46.

29. Ibid., p. 44.

30. Ibid., pp. 47–48.

31. Ibid., pp. 48–49.

32. Ibid., p. 48.

33. Ibid., p. 51.

34. Ibid.

35. Ibid.

36. Ibid., p. 53.

37. Ibid., pp. 54–55.

38. Ibid., p. 55.

39. Ibid., p. 56.

40. Ibid., p. 51.

41. Ibid., pp. 57–58.

42. Shipp, "Autobiography of 1930," p. 42.

43. Shipp, "Early Autobiography and Diary," p. 59.

44. Ibid.

45. Ibid., p. 61.

46. Ibid., pp. 61–62.

47. Ibid.

48. Ibid., p. 64.

49. Ibid.

50. Ibid.

51. Ibid.

52. Ibid., p. 65.
53. Ibid., p. 66.
54. Ibid.
55. Ibid.
56. Ibid.
57. Ibid., p. 68.
58. Ibid., pp. 68–69.
59. Ibid., p. 73.
60. Ibid., p. 75.
61. Ibid., p. 76.
62. Ibid., p. 77.
63. Ibid.
64. Ibid.
65. Ibid., p. 86.
66. Ibid.
67. Ibid., p. 87.
68. Ibid., p. 89.
69. Ibid.
70. Ibid., p. 91.
71. Ibid., p. 92.
72. Ibid., p. 93.
73. Ibid., p. 99.
74. Ibid., pp. 100–101.
75. Shipp, "Autobiography of 1930," introduction, p. iv.
76. Shipp, "Early Autobiography and Diary," p. 102.
77. Shipp, "Autobiography of 1930," pp. 29, 39.
78. Shipp, "Early Autobiography and Diary," p. 103.
79. Ibid.
80. Ibid., pp. 111–12.
81. Pearson, p. 17.
82. Ibid.
83. Shipp, "Early Autobiography and Diary," p. 118.
84. Ibid., p. 117.
85. Ibid., p. 115.
86. Ibid., p. 130.
87. McKinney, p. 4.
88. Shipp, "Early Autobiography and Diary," p. 132.
89. Ibid.
90. Ibid., p. 135.
91. *Utah Historical Quarterly* 49 (Summer 1981): 300–301.
92. Claire Noall, *Guardians of the Hearth* (Bountiful, Utah: Horizon Publishers, 1974), p. 97.

93. Ibid., p. 91.

94. Ibid., p. 97.

95. Ibid.

96. Keith Calvin Terry, "The Contributions of Medical Women During the First Fifty Years in Utah" (Master's thesis, Brigham Young University, 1964), p. 46.

97. Noall, p. 91.

98. Terry, p. 3.

99. Ibid., p. 37.

100. Noall, p. 95.

101. Ibid., p. 119.

102. Shipp, "Early Autobiography and Diary," p. 141.

103. Noall, p. 120.

104. Shipp, "Early Autobiography and Diary," p. 230.

Chapter 5

1. Ellis Reynolds Shipp, "Early Autobiography and Diary," p. 142.

2. Ibid.

3. Ibid., p. 144.

4. Ibid.

5. Ibid., p. 145.

6. Ibid., p. 146.

7. Ibid.

8. Ibid., p. 147.

9. Ibid., p. 148.

10. Ibid.

11. Ibid., p. 149.

12. Ibid., p. 151.

13. Ibid., p. 153.

14. Ibid., p. 157.

15. Ibid., p. 159.

16. Ibid., p. 156.

17. Ibid., p. 155.

18. Ibid., p. 160.

19. John Wanamaker, *Quaint Corners in Philadelphia* (Philadelphia and New York, 1883), p. 239.

20. Shipp, "Early Autobiography and Diary," p. 166.

21. Ibid., p. 162.

22. Ibid.

23. Ibid., p. 170.

24. Ibid., p. 171.
25. Ibid.
26. Ibid.
27. Ibid.
28. Wanamaker, p. 393.
29. Ibid.
30. Shipp, "Early Autobiography and Diary," p. 172.
31. Ibid.
32. Ibid., p. 175.
33. Ibid., p. 183.
34. Ibid., p. 182.
35. Ibid., p. 176.
36. Ibid.
37. Ibid., p. 179.
38. Ibid., p. 181.
39. Wanamaker, p. 394.
40. Shipp, "Early Autobiography and Diary," p. 181.
41. Ibid., p. 182.
42. Ibid., p. 184.
43. Ibid.
44. Ibid., p. 191.
45. Typed notes, Box B-4 (1967, 1973), Shipp Manuscript Collection.
46. Shipp, "Early Autobiography and Diary," p. 194.
47. Ibid.
48. Ibid., p. 195.
49. Ibid., p. 196.
50. Ibid.
51. Ibid., p. 197.
52. Ibid., pp. 197–98.
53. Ibid., p. 198.
54. Ibid., pp. 198–99.
55. Ibid., p. 199.

Chapter 6

1. Claire Noall, *Guardians of the Hearth*, p. 124.
2. Typed page, Shipp Manuscript Collection.
3. *Woman's Exponent* 5 (1 August 1876): 36.
4. Ibid.

5. Ibid.

6. Noall, p. 125.

7. Ibid.

8. Ellis Reynolds Shipp, "Early Autobiography and Diary," p. 200.

9. Ibid., p. 202.

10. Ibid.

11. Ibid.

12. Kate B. Carter, *An Enduring Legacy* (Salt Lake City: Daughters of the Utah Pioneers, 1946), p. 338.

13. Typed page, Shipp Manuscript Collection.

14. Shipp, "Early Autobiography and Diary," p. 205.

15. Ibid., pp. 205–6.

16. Ibid., p. 207.

17. Ibid., pp. 208–9.

18. Ibid., pp. 210–11.

19. Ibid., pp. 211–12.

20. Ibid., p. 213.

21. Miscellaneous notes on Ellis Reynolds Shipp by Olea Shipp Hill and Nellie Shipp McKinney, Shipp Manuscript Collection.

22. Shipp, "Early Autobiography and Diary," p. 220.

23. Ibid.

24. Ibid., p. 222.

25. Ibid.

26. Ibid., p. 225.

27. Ibid., p. 229.

28. Ibid., p. 230.

29. Ibid., pp. 231–32.

30. Ibid., pp. 233–34.

31. Ibid., p. 236.

32. Ibid.

33. Ellis Shipp Musser, ed., *The Early Autobiography and Diary of Ellis Reynolds Shipp, M.D.* (Salt Lake City: n.p., 1962), epigraph.

Chapter 7

1. Ellis Reynolds Shipp, "Autobiography of 1930," p. 52.

2. Ellis Reynolds Shipp, *Life Lines* (Salt Lake City: Skelton Publishing Co., 1910), p. 175.

3. Shipp, "Autobiography of 1930," p. 52.

4. Ibid.

5. Ibid.

6. Ibid.

7. "Introduction Sheet," p. 3; Shipp Manuscript Collection.

8. Ellis Reynolds Shipp to Milford Bard Shipp, 29 November 1874; Shipp Manuscript Collection.

9. Shipp, "Autobiography of 1930," p. 53.

10. Keith Calvin Terry, "The Contributions of Medical Women During the First Fifty Years in Utah," p. 52.

11. Ibid.

12. Shipp, "Autobiography of 1930," p. 54.

13. Ibid., p. 53.

14. Claire Noall, *Guardians of the Hearth*, p. 154.

15. Ibid.

16. Ibid., p. 155.

17. *History of the Relief Society, 1842–1966* (Salt Lake City: The General Board of the Relief Society of The Church of Jesus Christ of Latter-day Saints, 1966), p. 116.

18. Noall, p. 158.

19. *History of the Relief Society*, p. 116.

20. Shipp, "Autobiography of 1930," p. 54.

21. Noall, p. 160.

22. Ibid.

23. Shipp, "Autobiography of 1930," p. 56.

24. Ibid., p. 55.

25. Handwritten sheet, Shipp Manuscript Collection.

26. Typed sheet, Shipp Manuscript Collection.

27. Ibid.

28. Ibid.

29. Bardella Shipp Curtis, "Dr. Milford Bard Shipp—Highlights," p. 2; Shipp Manuscript Collection.

30. Ibid.

31. Shipp, "Autobiography of 1930," p. 57.

32. Ibid.

33. Ibid.

34. Ibid.

35. *Woman's Exponent* 16 (15 March 1888): 156.

36. Shipp, "Autobiography of 1930," p. 53.

37. Nellie Shipp McKinney, "Historical Sketch of Milford Bard Shipp," p. 6; Shipp Manuscript Collection.

38. Curtis, p. 3.

39. Ibid., p. 2.

40. *Salt Lake Sanitarian*, April 1888, p. 14.

41. Noall, p. 160.

42. Ibid., p. 161.

43. Ibid.

44. *Salt Lake Sanitarian*, June 1888, front page insignia.

45. Ibid., July 1888, p. 111.

46. Ibid., June 1888, p. 33.

47. Ibid., July 1888, pp. 109, 111.

48. Ibid., November 1888, p. 181; July 1888, p. 111.

Chapter 8

1. Ellis Reynolds Shipp, *Life Lines*, pp. 107–8.

2. Ellis Reynolds Shipp, sketch entitled "Woman in Medicine," p. 1; Shipp Manuscript Collection.

3. Ibid., p. 3.

4. Ibid., p. 5.

5. Ellis Shipp Musser, in preface to Ellis Reynolds Shipp, "Early Autobiography and Diary," p. 2; Shipp Manuscript Collection.

6. Ellis Reynolds Shipp, "Autobiography of 1930," p. 53.

7. Kate B. Carter, *An Enduring Legacy*, p. 339.

8. Terry, "The Contributions of Medical Women During the First Fifty Years in Utah," p. 7.

9. *Young Woman's Journal*, January 1897, pp. 391–92.

10. Ibid., p. 392.

11. Ibid., p. 391.

12. Musser, p. 4.

13. Ibid.

14. Ibid., p. 5.

15. Shipp, "Autobiography of 1930," p. 54.

16. Ibid., p. 55.

17. Ibid.

18. Ibid.

19. Ibid.

20. Miscellaneous handwritten notes by Olea Shipp Hill, p. 4; Shipp Manuscript Collection.

21. Ibid., p. 5.

22. Ibid., pp. 5–6.

23. J. Sterling Morton, *History of Nebraska, Illustrated* (Lincoln, Nebr.: Western Publishing and Engraving Co., 1906), p. 131.

24. Ibid., pp. 131–32.

25. Shipp, *Life Lines*, pp. 32–34.

26. Typed page, Shipp Manuscript Collection.

27. Ellis Reynolds Shipp, "Life of William Fletcher Reynolds, Utah Pioneer of 1852," p. 4; Shipp Manuscript Collection.

28. Emmeline B. Wells, in introduction to Shipp, *Life Lines.*

29. Ibid.

30. Shipp, *Life Lines,* title page.

31. Shipp, *Life Lines,* dedication.

32. Nellie Shipp McKinney, "Historical Sketch of Milford Bard Shipp," p. 6.

33. Ellis Reynolds Shipp to Milford Bard Shipp, 3 March 1918, Shipp Manuscript Collection.

Chapter 9

1. Handwritten sheet by Olea Shipp Hill, Shipp Manuscript Collection.

2. Ellis Reynolds Shipp to her son Richard, 15 July 1921, Shipp Manuscript Collection.

3. Ibid.

4. Ellis Reynolds Shipp to her daughter Ellis, 24 July 1917, Shipp Manuscript Collection.

5. Ellis Reynolds Shipp, *Life Lines,* p. 246.

6. Ellis Reynolds Shipp to her children, 4 January 1933, Shipp Manuscript Collection.

7. Handwritten sheets, Shipp Manuscript Collection.

8. Ellis Reynolds Shipp, journal entry, 2 June 1936, Shipp Manuscript Collection.

9. Ibid., November 1936.

10. Ibid.

11. Ibid.

12. Typed sheet, Shipp Manuscript Collection.

13. Shipp, journal entry, March 1936.

14. Ellis Reynolds Shipp, "Early Autobiography and Diary," p. 86.

15. Shipp, *Life Lines,* pp. 199–200.

16. Typed sheet, Shipp Manuscript Collection.

17. Ibid.

18. Ibid.

19. Excerpt from speech by Annie Wells Cannon at funeral services for Ellis Reynolds Shipp, 5 February 1939, Shipp Manuscript Collection.

20. Excerpt from sermon by George Albert Smith at funeral services for Ellis Reynolds Shipp, 5 February 1939, Shipp Manuscript Collection.

21. Typed sheet, Shipp Manuscript Collection.

22. *Relief Society Magazine*, March 1939, p. 194.

23. *Salt Lake Telegram*, 2 February 1939.

24. Ibid.

25. Typed sheet, Shipp Manuscript Collection.

26. Ibid.

27. *Deseret News*, 10 November 1932, p. 1.

28. Ellis Reynolds Shipp, "Autobiography of 1930," p. 53.

29. Handwritten sheet, Shipp Manuscript Collection.

30. Typed sheet, Shipp Manuscript Collection.

31. Ernest L. Wilkinson, *Dedication and Naming of 22 Buildings* (Provo, Utah: Brigham Young University, 1954), p. 40.

32. Kate B. Carter, *An Enduring Legacy*, pp. 339–40.

33. Handwritten sheet by Olea Shipp Hill, Shipp Manuscript Collection.

34. Shipp, *Life Lines*, p. 40.

35. Shipp, "Autobiography of 1930," p. 59.

Bibliography

Primary Source Material

Ellis Reynolds Shipp Manuscript Collection,
Utah State Historical Society, Salt Lake City, Utah

Curtis, Bardella Shipp. "Dr. Milford Bard Shipp — Highlights."

McKinney, Nellie Shipp. "Historical Sketch of Milford Bard Shipp."

Pearson, Sarah Ellis Hawley. "A Sketch of Our Beloved and Honored Pioneers of the Hawley Family."

Shipp, Ellis Reynolds, "Early Autobiography and Diary."

————. "Autobiography of 1930."

————. Miscellaneous materials, Box B-4. 1967, 1973.

Secondary Source Material

Arrington, Leonard J. "The Economic Role of Pioneer Mormon Women." *Western Humanities Review* 9 (Spring 1955): 145 – 64.

Burton, Alma P. *Karl G. Maeser, Mormon Educator.* Salt Lake City: Deseret Book Company, 1953.

Carter, Kate B. *An Enduring Legacy.* Vol. 7 of *Heart Throbs of the West.* Salt Lake City: Daughters of the Utah Pioneers, 1946.

Ellsworth, S. George. *Utah's Heritage.* Salt Lake City and Santa Barbara, Calif.: Peregrine Smith, 1977.

Grua, Suzanna Mae Clark. *Brief History of Pleasant Grove, Utah.* N.p., n.d.

History of the Relief Society, 1842–1966. Salt Lake City: The General Board of the Relief Society of The Church of Jesus Christ of Latter-day Saints, 1966.

Kane, Mrs. Thomas L. *Twelve Mormon Homes.* Dallas and Philadelphia: L. K. Taylor Publishing Co., 1874.

Maughan, Ila Fisher. *Pioneer Theatre in the Desert.* Salt Lake City: Deseret Book Company, 1961.

Memories That Live: A Centennial History of Utah County. Salt Lake City: Daughters of the Utah Pioneers, 1947.

Morton, J. Sterling. *History of Nebraska, Illustrated.* Lincoln, Nebr.: Western Publishing and Engraving Co., 1906.

Noall, Sandra H. "Nursing in Utah." Ellis Reynolds Shipp Manuscript Collection, Utah State Historical Society.

Noall, Claire. *Guardians of the Hearth.* Bountiful, Utah: Horizon Publishers, 1974.

Rose, Blanche E. "History of Medicine in Utah." May 1939. Ellis Reynolds Shipp Manuscript Collection, Utah State Historical Society.

Shipp, Ellis Reynolds. *Life Lines*. Salt Lake City: Skelton Publishing Co., 1910.

Spencer, Clarissa Young, and Harmer, Mabel. *Brigham Young at Home*. Salt Lake City: Deseret Book Company, 1963.

Terry, Keith Calvin. "The Contributions of Medical Women During the First Fifty Years in Utah." Master's thesis, Brigham Young University, 1964.

Walker, Lucile Harvey, and Smith, Fern Eyring. "Pleasant Grove." Manuscript Collection, Pleasant Grove Public Library, Pleasant Grove, Utah.

Wanamaker, John. *Quaint Corners in Philadelphia*. Philadelphia and New York, 1883.

Wilkinson, Ernest L. *Dedication and Naming of 22 Buildings*. Dedicatory pamphlet. Provo, Utah: Brigham Young University, 1954.

Wilson, William M. *Utah County, Utah, in Pictures and Prose*. N.p., 1914.

Periodicals

Deseret News
Relief Society Magazine
Salt Lake Sanitarian
Salt Lake Telegram
Utah Historical Quarterly
Woman's Exponent
Young Woman's Journal

Index

Hawley, Susan Ellis (cousin of ERS), 7, 20
Hawley, William (grandfather of ERS): maple
    sugar business, 1–2; innkeeper, 2; de-
    parted from Canada, 3; ERS's illness,
    3–4; conversion, 5–6; wood contract,
    6; emigrating family, 7; crossed plains,
    7–11; Battle Creek homestead, 13;
    alderman, 14; excommunicated, 47; ERS
    visited, 54, 58; plural marriage, 75;
    Pleasant Grove hotel, 78; rebaptized, 96;
    good spirit, 108; death, 141–42
Hayne, Julia Dean, 54
Health, 90
Heaven, visits to, 29
Henderson County, Illinois, 6
Hillstead, Elizabeth. *See* Shipp, Elizabeth
    "Lizzie"
Hillstead family, 80
Holy Cross Hospital, 142
Home missionaries, 36
Horne, M. Isabella, 156
Household chores, 17
Hybette, Lide, 33
Hyde, Orson, 96

— I —

Indians, on the plains, 9
Ink, 19
International Council of Women, 148

— J —

Jacobs, Chariton, 49, 53–54
Jacobs, Zebulon, 33–35, 48, 51
Jefferson Medical College, 140

— K —

Kimball, Heber C., 66
Kimball, Sarah, 93

— L —

Lamb, Polly, 8
Larsen, Christina. *See* Reynolds, Christina
Lehi, Utah, 11
Life Lines, 167
Lion House, 50
Lund, Anthon, 39, 42

— M —

MacArthur, Duncan, 12–13
MacArthur, Susan, 26

McClean, Mary Ann, 142–43
McKenzie, David, 56
McRae, Alexander, 69
Maeser, Karl G., 52–53, 55
Maple sugar, 2
Marget, Phil, 56
Marriage, 94
Married couples, exemplary, 30
Mayhew, "Cal," 36, 67
Mayhew, Lydia, 23–24, 42. *See also*
    Robinson, Lydia
Mayhew, Otto, 58
Midwifery, 100
Molasses mills, 13
Mormon Battalion, party, 51
Mount Pleasant, Utah, 39, 45–46
Mushrooms, 15
Musser, Ellis, 183–85. *See also* Shipp, Ellis

— N —

North Antelope Mining Company, 171
Nurses, 156, 158

— P —

Parades, 16
Paul, Martha Hughes, 139
Peach-paring parties, 36
Pearson, Sarah, 157
Philadelphia, Pennsylvania, 110
Pioneer Memorial Museum, 184
Pioneers: emigration, 7–11; food scarcity,
    15; home life, 11–12, 17; Iowa reaction
    to, 5
Pleasant Grove, Utah, 12–14, 47, 78, 93.
    See also Battle Creek, Utah
Plural marriage: acceptance of, 74–75;
    children, 80; happiness, 82–83; life-
    styles, 88–89; rationale, 101; sister
    wives, 80–82; to deceased women, 89;
    wives notified of, 74
Polygamy. *See* Plural marriage
Pratt, Romania, 101, 107–8, 113, 130, 139
Prophecies, rain, 46
Provo River bridge, 13

— R —

Reynolds, Anna (mother of ERS): marriage,
    1; death of infant, 4; baptism, 6; bond
    with ERS, 16–18; industriousness, 17;
    illness, 28; death, 29